THIRD EDITION

REFLECTIVE TEACHING

Professional Artistry Through Inquiry

James G. Henderson

Kent State University

Merrill
Prentice Hall

Upper Saddle River, New Jersey
Columbus, Ohio

Library of Congress Cataloging-in-Publication Data

Reflective teaching: professional artistry through inquiry/ [edited by] James G. Henderson.—3rd ed.

    p. cm.

    Rev. ed. of: Reflective teaching. 2nd ed. c1996.

    Includes bibliographical references and index.

    ISBN 0-13-025846-6

       1. Teaching. 2. Teaching—Case studies. 3. Inquiry (Theory of knowledge) I. Henderson, James George. II. Reflective teaching.

LB1025.3 .R437 2001

371.102—dc21

                                                      00-028751

Vice President and Publisher: Jeffery W. Johnston
Executive Editor: Debra A. Stollenwerk
Editorial Assistant: Penny S. Burleson
Production Editor: Linda H. Bayma
Production Coordination: WordCrafters Editorial Services, Inc.
Design Coordinator: Diane C. Lorenzo
Photo Coordinator: Anthony Magnacca
Cover Designer: Thomas Borah
Cover art: © SuperStock
Production Manager: Pamela D. Bennett
Director of Marketing: Kevin Flanagan
Marketing Manager: Amy June
Marketing Services Manager: Krista Groshong

This book was set in ITC Garamond by Carlisle Communications, Ltd. It was printed and bound by R.R. Donnelley & Sons Company. The cover was printed by Phoenix Color Corp.

Earlier edition, entitled *Reflective Teaching: Becoming an Inquiring Educator,* © 1992 by Macmillan Publishing Company.

Photo Credits: Pages 2, 34, 68, 110, 130, 150: Anthony Magnacca/Merrill; p. 172: Barbara Schwartz/Merrill.

Merrill
Prentice Hall

10 9 8 7 6 5 4 3 2 1
ISBN 0-13-025846-6

This book is dedicated to John Dewey, who perhaps more than any other educational philosopher understood the importance of teaching for democratic living. As we enter the twenty-first century, we should keep in mind what John Dewey wrote in "My Pedagogic Creed" at the dawn of the twentieth century:

> I believe . . . that the teacher is engaged, not simply in the training of individuals, but in the formation of the proper social life. . . . Every teacher should realize the dignity of his [or her] calling; that he [or she] is a social servant set apart for the maintenance of proper social order and the securing of the right social growth. In this way the teacher always is the prophet. . . . The art of thus giving shape to human powers and adapting them to social service is the supreme art; one calling into its service the best of artists . . . no insight, sympathy, tact, executive power is too great for such service. (J. Flinders & S. J. Thornton [Eds.] *The Curriculum Studies Reader* [New York: Routledge, 1997], 23).

This book is also dedicated to my parents, both of whom are highly committed teachers who understand the importance of educating for quality of living.

FOREWORD

ESCAPING THE BIG BOX: INQUIRY AS DEMOCRATIC PRACTICE

We recently shared Toni Morrison's (1999) wonderful new book, *The Big Box*. The book spoke to us in profound ways about what it means to live an inquiring life as a teacher; what it means to create school contexts where, as teachers, we can live inquiring lives with students; and what it means to create spaces in our classrooms where we work to help our students experience democracy as a way of living. The themes that Morrison introduces in her story of children confined in boxes came to mind quickly as we read the pages of *Reflective Teaching: Professional Artistry Through Inquiry*. Henderson dedicates this book to John Dewey and writes for an audience of educators who want to help their students experience democracy on a daily basis.

In this foreword we interweave a retelling of Morrison's book with themes emerging from Henderson's book and with the wonders raised by inquiring into our own lives as teachers. Morrison's book tells a story of three children—Patty, Mickey and Liza Sue—who do not fit easily into the world—a world often constructed at a distance from, and inattentive to, their hopes and imaginings. One of the most compelling segments of *The Big Box* involves Patty in a child's story of school. Patty is described as a typical child who lives in a nearby house. She has a problem, however; she has too much fun in school. She makes her teachers nervous by talking, singing, going to the bathroom too often, running in the halls, and refusing to play with dolls. Her behavior results in a meeting during which her teachers deliberate on possible cures. While they agree she has potential, she needs to learn to follow the rules. Her teachers and her parents agree that Patty just can't handle her freedom.

As Morrison's story and the images surrounding it drew us into Patty's world, we began to wonder:

- ✎ What school stories are written for children? For teachers?

- ✎ Whose knowing matters?

- ✎ Without relational negotiation, how are these school stories experienced by children? By teachers?

- ✎ Who are the children locked into these school stories?

- ✎ What becomes not seen, not heard, not understood about children's storied lives?

- ✎ Does students' "absence" from knowing their lives matter to those who tell official stories about the quality of schools?

Not unlike the threads woven across the chapters in Henderson's book, we heard in Patty's response to her teachers a yearning for the negotiation of democracy, a kind of negotiation attentive to each person's knowing.

In Morrison's book, Patty sits and listens with bowed head to her teachers' pronouncements on her inability to handle her freedom. She reminds her teachers that she folds her clothes, eats her vegetables, washes her face, and cleans her nails. She tells them that she does not want to be rude, but that she wants to keep her freedom. She acknowledges that her teachers are trying to do what is best for her. But, she concludes, if they handle freedom their way, then, in Morrison's words, "It's not my freedom or free." Patty's response created additional wonders for us:

- ✎ Distanced from children's experience, what stories are we living?

- ✎ Are we awake to context, to selves, to complexity, to multiplicity, to tensions?

- ✎ To whom does freedom belong?

Patty's pleas are to no avail and the teachers place her in Morrison's metaphorical big brown box with lovely furniture, toys, clothes, and food, but with a securely locked door. The refrain that runs throughout the book ends with a line that says that those kids cannot handle their freedom.

Who are "those" kids, we wondered. Who are we in relation with them? Attending closely to the space of the big brown box, we wondered:

- What are the locks that so profoundly shape our contexts?
- Who constructs the locks?
- Who places the locks there?
- Who defines the qualities of such locked spaces?
- How do these qualities shape the lives and experiences of the teachers and children trapped within them?

Morrison's book called us to ask ourselves, as teachers, many of the questions that the conceptual framework of this book wants us to engage with: questions that emerge from public moral inquiry, multiperspective inquiry, deliberative inquiry, autobiographical inquiry, and critical inquiry. As we played with the questions that Morrison's text called us to ask of ourselves, still more wonders came forward. These wonders resonated across the kinds of inquiry Henderson proposes:

- In such places of normalization, what are the possibilities for wide-awakeness?
- What might be in places where disruption and difference are attended to?
- What happens to selves who help to shape such disruptions?
- What are we afraid of that makes us search to "cure," to box in, to deny such hopeful counterstories?
- What possibilities lay beyond the walls, the borders constructed by boxes?

If we become inquiring practitioners who, as Henderson points out, recognize that there is no more important work "in our democratic society than helping students realize their capacities to live as free and responsible citizens," might we, like Patty, Mickey, and Liza Sue eventually learn how to break free of the boxes constraining ourselves and the selves of others? What new possibilities might we awaken to?

Henderson's book is filled with stories of teachers who are trying to engage in inquiry into their practices, who are trying to live out stories in which they break out of Morrison's metaphorical boxes to engage themselves and the students with whom they work, in learning to live stories of freedom, of democracy. To learn to engage in these kinds of inquiry is an ongoing learning task, an important part of professional practice. In the stories in this book, many possible ways of learning how to do this work are told. These teachers' stories call us to join with them in composing inquiring lives. As we learn to tell our stories of inquiry, we, too, will find others to join us in breaking out of the big boxes in which all of us—like Patty, Mickey, and Liza Sue—are trapped. Together we can begin to recompose our stories of school.

D. Jean Clandinin
Janice Huber
Karen Whelan

Centre for Research for Teacher Education and Development University of Alberta

REFERENCE

Morrison, Toni (with Slade Morrison). (1999). *The big box*. New York: Hyperion Books for Children.

PREFACE

This third edition of *Reflective Teaching* has been written to support the professional inquiries of teachers who see themselves as more than content specialists. The book's focus is stated in its opening two sentences: "Perhaps you know a special kind of teacher. This is an educator who understands that his or her job is not just teaching subject matter but *teaching a way of living*." This way of living is understood as the practice of a *generative and generous intellect*. John Dewey's phrase for this understanding of the "good life" was *learning through experience,* which he felt provided the basic moral justification for a democratic society:

> The question I would raise concerns why we prefer democratic and humane arrangements to those which are autocratic and harsh. And by "why," I mean the *reason* for preferring them. . . . Can we find any reason that does not ultimately come down to the belief that democratic social arrangements promote a better quality of human experience, one which is more widely accessible and enjoyed, than do non-democratic and anti-democratic forms of social life? Does not the principle of regard for individual freedom and for decency and kindliness of human relations come back in the end to the conviction that these things are tributary to a higher quality of experience on the part of a greater number than are methods of repression and coercion or force? Is it not the reason for our preference that we believe that mutual consultation and convictions reached through persuasion, make possible a better quality of experience than can otherwise be provided on any wide scale? (Dewey, 1998/1938, pp. 24–26; author's emphasis)

This book builds on this progressive understanding of the "good" life. Current and future teachers receive guidance on how to integrate five forms of inquiry into the continuing reflections on their craft so that they are better able to facilitate a *democratic living* that is manifested through the daily practice of a generative and generous intellect. These five forms of professional study are: public moral inquiry, multiperspective inquiry, deliberative inquiry, autobiographical inquiry, and critical inquiry. Because this is a very sophisticated and challenging approach to *reflective teaching,* each form of inquiry is carefully introduced through the use of an illustrative vignette, a concise explanation, a set of guiding questions, and an experienced teacher narrative. This four-part strategy, which has been field-tested with a voluntary group of education students, provides a number of ways to understand the inquiry material in this book.

Though the purpose of this book is to present five forms of professional inquiry, the text ends with a discussion of *teacher leadership.* There is a reason for this conclusion. Teachers can better develop their inquiry capacities by working with their peers in a supportive and respectful manner. Initiating such professional collaboration will require the efforts of "lead" teachers working in conjunction with school administrators and other educational stakeholders. The history of education in the twentieth century includes many stories of teachers leading the fight for socially respectable salaries and benefits. Hopefully, the history of education in the twenty-first century will include many stories of teachers leading the fight for a work life of socially responsible professional inquiry.

New to This Edition

To ensure the readability of this edition of *Reflective Teaching,* we have added:

§   Useful tables, schematics, and lists

§   A careful analysis of craft reflection and five forms of professional inquiry

§   A concise definition of professional inquiry artistry and teacher leadership

§   Numerous illustrative vignettes and teacher narratives

§ The integration of guiding questions for inquiry and discussion in each chapter

Acknowledgments

Thanks to Mary Jo Marksz for her collaborative assistance with chapter 2 and to Sharon Klimm for her assistance with chapters 4 and 5. Thanks also to Richard Hawthorne and Jan Wolf for their editorial assistance. Finally, we appreciate the input received from the following reviewers: Scot Danforth, University of Missouri–St. Louis; James G. Hademenos, Angelo State University; Stephen Lafer, University of Nevada, Reno; Charlene S. Newman, Kent State University; and Joy Faini Saab, West Virginia University.

REFERENCE

Dewey, J. (1998). *Experience and education: The 60th anniversary edition*. West Lafayette, IN: Kappa Delta Pi. (Original work published 1938)

CONTRIBUTING AUTHORS

The following individuals served as contributing authors for this book. Those who contributed to the text's background discussions on professional inquiry and teacher leadership are listed first, followed by those who contributed case narratives. The authors of the narratives are also footnoted at the beginning of each case.

Background Discussions

Chapter 3   Mary Styslinger

Chapter 4   Laura Kincaid

Chapter 5   Catherine Hackney

Chapter 6   Jennifer Mahon and Ray Timlin

Chapter 7   Rebecca McElfresh

Case Narratives

Chapter 1   Jan Wolf

Chapter 2   Bridget Robbins

Chapter 3   Mary Styslinger

Chapter 4   Patricia Armstrong

Chapter 5   Tebra Stepnicka

Chapter 6   Natalie Sekicky

Chapter 7   Carol Chiorian

DISCOVER THE COMPANION WEBSITE
ACCOMPANYING THIS BOOK

The Prentice Hall Companion Website:
A Virtual Learning Environment

Technology is a constantly growing and changing aspect of our field that is creating a need for content and resources. To address this emerging need, Prentice Hall has developed an online learning environment for students and professors alike—Companion Websites—to support our textbooks.

In creating a Companion Website, our goal is to build on and enhance what the textbook already offers. For this reason, the content for each user-friendly website is organized by topic and provides the professor and student with a variety of meaningful resources. Common features of a Companion Website include:

For the Professor—

Every Companion Website integrates **Syllabus Manager**™, an online syllabus creation and management utility.

§ **Syllabus Manager**™ provides you, the instructor, with an easy, step-by-step process to create and revise syllabi, with direct links into Companion Website and other online content without having to learn HTML.

§ Students may logon to your syllabus during any study session. All they need to know is the web address for the Companion Website and the password you've assigned to your syllabus.

§ After you have created a syllabus using **Syllabus Manager**™, students may enter the syllabus for their course section from any point in the Companion Website.

§   Clicking on a date, the student is shown the list of activities for the assignment. The activities for each assignment are linked directly to actual content, saving time for students.

§   Adding assignments consists of clicking on the desired due date, then filling in the details of the assignment—name of the assignment, instructions, and whether or not it is a one-time or repeating assignment.

§   In addition, links to other activities can be created easily. If the activity is online, a URL can be entered in the space provided, and it will be linked automatically in the final syllabus.

§   Your completed syllabus is hosted on our servers, allowing convenient updates from any computer on the Internet. Changes you make to your syllabus are immediately available to your students at their next logon.

For the Student—

§   **Topic Overviews**—outline key concepts in topic areas

§   **Electronic Bluebook**—send homework or essays directly to your instructor's email with this paperless form

§   **Message Board**—serves as a virtual bulletin board to post—or respond to—questions or comments to/from a national audience

§   **Chat**—real-time chat with anyone who is using the text anywhere in the country—ideal for discussion and study groups, class projects, etc.

§   **Web Destinations**—links to www sites that relate to each topic area

§   **Professional Organizations**—links to organizations that relate to topic areas

§   **Additional Resources**—access to topic-specific content that enhances material found in the text

To take advantages of these and other resources, please visit the *Reflective Teaching: Professional Artistry Through Inquiry,* Third Edition, Companion Website at
www.prenhall.com/henderson

BRIEF CONTENTS

CONTENTS

Chapter 4
Deliberative Inquiry   111

Chapter 5
Autobiographical Inquiry   131

Chapter 6
Critical Inquiry   151

Chapter 7
Transformative Teacher Leadership   173

Appendix
The Teacher-Character Ideological Map 195

REFLECTIVE
TEACHING

CHAPTER 1

PROFESSIONAL ARTISTRY THROUGH INQUIRY

§

INTRODUCTION

Perhaps you know a special kind of teacher. This is an educator who understands that his or her job is not just teaching subject matter but *teaching a way of living.* If you have experienced such a professional, you are indeed fortunate. They have helped you discover purpose and meaning in your life. Without them, your life would be qualitatively different: less loving, less productive, less. . . . You complete the sentence. We never forget such teachers. And perhaps at some point in our adult years, we mail them a note of gratitude or unexpectedly meet them in a public space like a restaurant and thank them personally. This book is inspired by a special group of such teachers: ***those educators who help their students experience democracy as a way of living.***

To be a teacher in a society with democratic ideals is a noble calling. You are to be congratulated for choosing a challenging professional vocation that is vital to the health of constitutional democracies. When you work to nurture *democratic living* in your classroom, you provide an essential public service. When you teach in this way, the social value of your educational efforts can be favorably compared to the work of a judge defending the rights of a group of devalued citizens. You may have encountered family members or friends who have challenged your decision to become a teacher. Your best response to their skepticism or cynicism is the professional inquiry focus of this book. Tell them that you have dedicated yourself to the challenge of facilitating students' direct *experience* of our society's *democratic ideals.* Then ask them this question, *"What work is more important in our democratic society than helping students realize their capacities to live as free and responsible adults?"*

This book begins with an introduction to three *basics* of democratic living. You have undoubtedly encountered the expression, "back to basics." People who use this phrase, usually conservatives, are calling for a renewed educational emphasis on basic skills. Think of this book as a "forward to basics" text. You will be studying three important basics for living productively in a pluralistic society with democratic ideals. Because these basics are not, at this historical moment, well established in our society, they are based on a "forward" visionary and progressive educational orientation. You will then learn how these three basics can be applied to education. You will be presented with an overview of a particular type of *s*ubject, *s*elf, and *s*ocial learning—the *3S's* of teaching for democratic living.

The next section of this chapter sets the stage for the rest of the book. You will be introduced in a commonsensical way to continuously reflect on your teaching craft, and you will learn that educators who integrate five *forms of inquiry* into their continuing reflections are developing their ability to *teach for democratic living.* The word *artistry* traces back to the old Latin term *ars. Ars* means "putting things together; joining." You are learning a type of professional artistry in this book, hence this text's subtitle: *Professional Artistry through Inquiry.* You are, literally, learning to "join together" five forms of inquiry with your craft reflections. These forms of inquiry will be called: *public moral inquiry, multiperspective inquiry, deliberative inquiry, autobiographical inquiry,* and *critical inquiry.* As you are introduced to these five ways to professionally inquire, you will read why each one is important to the challenge of teaching for democratic living.

THREE BASICS OF DEMOCRATIC LIVING

The philosophy of *democratic living* is informed by three basic moral precepts. *The first precept is that human affairs are best conducted through* **intelligence** *rather than through* *either* **habit** *or* **force.** Dewey (1936) argues that this principle is particularly important when a society is undergoing fundamental changes:

> The feeling that social change of any basic character can be brought about only by violent force is the product of lack of faith in intelligence as a method and this loss of faith is in large measure the product of a schooling, that because of its comparatively unfree condition, has not enabled youth to face intelligently the realities of our social life, political and economic.
>
> There are ultimately but three forces that control society—habit, coercive and violent force, and action directed by intelligence. In fairly normal times, habit and custom are by far the strongest force. . . . [During times of social upheaval,] reactionaries who strive to prevent any change of the old order . . . [may have] the power that enables them to use brute force in its less overt forms: by coercion, by intimidation, and by various forms of indirect pressure. . . .
>
> Training for good citizenship is one thing when conditions are simple and fairly stable. It is quite another when conditions are confused, complicated, and unsettled, when class divisions and struggles are imminent. Every force that operates to limit the freedom of education is a premium put upon ultimate violence to effect needed change. Every force that tends to liberate educational processes is a premium placed upon intelligent and orderly methods of directing to a more just, equitable, and humane end the social changes that are going on anyway. (p. 166)

To educate for *democratic living* requires teachers to cultivate their students' capacities to engage in "intelligent" learning activities. They must daily find creative, responsible ways to challenge their students' inclinations to unthinkingly adopt habits and customs or submit to force. In his book, *To Think,* Frank Smith (1990) provides a concise analysis of human intelligence. He provides an alphabetized list of seventy-seven thinking terms, beginning with "analyze" and ending with "wonder." His list has been reproduced in Figure 1.1. After presenting an overview of the breadth and depth of the human intellect, Smith concentrates his discussion on several key topics, including the nature of commonplace, creative, and critical thinking. Teachers who educate for *democratic living* find texts like Smith's to be helpful guides.

analyze	conjecture	fabricate	organize	review
anticipate	consider	fantasize	plan	revise
apprehend	contemplate	foresee	plot	ruminate
argue	create	guess	ponder	schematize
assert	deduce	hypothesize	postulate	scheme
assume	deem	imagine	predict	speculate
attend	deliberate	induce	premeditate	suggest
believe	determine	infer	presume	suppose
calculate	devise	intend	presuppose	suspect
categorize	discover	introspect	project	systematize
classify	divine	invent	propose	theorize
cogitate	empathize	judge	rationalize	understand
comprehend	estimate	know	reason	· wonder
conceive	examine	meditate	recall	
concentrate	expect	muse	reflect	
conceptualize	explain	opine	remember	

Figure 1.1
Seventy-Seven Thinking Words

They are aware that they must possess a well-developed understanding of the human intellect, particularly as applied to the subjects they teach, if they are to do their work properly.

The second precept of ***democratic living*** is as important as the first. ***Humans must use their intellect for generative purposes.*** To be *generative* is to embrace the love of human growth. According to Dewey (1932/1985), a generative educational experience allows for the continuous "development and fulfillment of self, while [its contrast] . . . stunts and starves selfhood by cutting it off from the connections necessary to its growth" (p. 302). In a poetic evocation of Dewey's philosophy of continuous growth, Garrison (1997) writes: "Those who are in love with life desire to grow. Those who love to grow, love and care for others, and let others care for them. That is the paradoxical logic of expansive growth. Only the truly tough-minded dare embrace this paradoxical truth" (p. 52). Garrison (1997) notes that *generativity* is closely linked to creativity: "Growth means the continued creation and creative unification of meanings and values. Evil is the decay of those values that sustain life and growth. Growth is the all-inclusive and supreme value because artistic creation . . . is the most magnificent activity of the living creature" (p. 49).

The third precept of *democratic living* is closely related to the second. **Humans must use their intellect for generous purposes.** To be *generous* is to be sensitive to others' beliefs, styles, and circumstances. Meier (1997) provides an elegant account of this human virtue:

> Well-developed empathy makes it hard to feel untouched by the misery of others; it enables us to hear their voices inside our own head and to understand their explanations and their "side" of the story. Reading the newspaper, for example, thus becomes both more compelling and more difficult. Empathy makes us want to run toward and away from at the same time. In imagining ourselves in the shoes of others, the world gets reshaped before our eyes in a way that is both thrilling and uncomfortable. Home—wherever we started out—is changed forever by this encounter with the "other." Empathy subtly broadens our capacity for imagination; our natural childish playfulness is expanded, not obliterated. Good literature, great drama, and powerful art of every kind—all these help a person to develop empathy. Such is the purpose of a good education for democracy. (p. 63)

In her philosophical essay, *The Dialectic of Freedom,* Maxine Greene (1988) provides insight into the nature of the *generative* and *generous intellect.* She argues that people who develop themselves in this way reject "oppression or exploitation or segregation or neglect" while engaging in authentic creative activities with others (p. 9). Her book is, ultimately, a celebration of such life-affirming individuals:

> Looking back, we can discern individuals in their we-relations with others, inserting themselves in the world by means of projects, embarking on new beginnings in spaces they open themselves. We can recall them—Thomas Jefferson, the Grimké sisters, Susan B. Anthony, Jane Addams, Frederick Douglass, W. E. B. DuBois, Martin Luther King, John Dewey, Carol Gilligan, Nel Noddings, Mary Daly—opening spaces where freedom is the mainspring, where people create themselves by acting in concert. (p. 134)

When teachers invite their students to study topics of oppression, exploitation, segregation, and neglect, they are encouraging their students to use their intellectual powers in generative and generous ways. They are *teaching for democratic living*. In parallel fashion, when teachers invite their students to collaborate on creative and meaningful learning projects, they are also encouraging their students to use their intellectual powers in generative and generous ways. They are also *teaching for democratic living*. Concerning the value of personally meaningful human growth, Noddings (1997) writes:

> If kids are occupied in legitimate studies connected to their own life stories, if they see themselves in what they are asked to do, then they are likely to acquire both the confidence and the skills to learn new material. Therefore they will not be "trapped." Cherished for who they are in every educational setting, they will learn how "to become" and how to learn. (pp. 56–57)

THE 3S's OF TEACHING FOR DEMOCRATIC LIVING

The three "basics" of democratic living can be directly applied to student learning. Valuing *intelligence* over habit or force highlights the significance of thoughtful subject matter learning. Valuing *generativity* advances the idea that students should learn to see themselves as active lifelong learners, while valuing *generosity* underscores the importance of respecting human diversity. These three student learning considerations can be characterized as the *3S's* of *teaching for democratic living*. The 3S's refer to (1) thoughtful *s*ubject learning, (2) learning to see one-*s*elf as a lifelong learner, and (3) learning to interact *s*ocially with diverse others. Table 1.1 summarizes the application of the three precepts of democratic living to student learning.

Table 1.1

Basic Moral Precepts	Student Learning Application
Intellect	Thoughtful Subject Learning
Generativity	Self as Lifelong Learner
Generosity	Social Interaction with Diverse Others

Students' Subject Learning

Teaching for democratic living requires the use of ***thinking-centered, performance-based*** activities. Perkins (1993/1994) describes a thinking-centered lesson as engaging "students in a lot of thinking about the content that they are learning" (p. 84). He then states that thinking-centered learning can occur in a variety of ways including:

- Classroom discussion around thought-demanding questions.

- Peer teaching, where students must think through a topic carefully in order to teach it to other students.

- Collaborative learning, where students share responsibility for learning something and must organize themselves and the topic to do it well.

- Problem-based learning, where students study content by seeking out the information needed to solve problems.

- Project-based learning, where students gain context knowledge through complex, often socially meaningful projects.

- Engagements in "understanding performances," which ask students to think with what they know in order to demonstrate and build their understanding.

- Infusion of critical and creative thinking into subject matter instruction, where students analyze, critique, defend, ask what-if questions, and explore alternative points of view.

- Use of authentic problems that have real-world significance and a messy open-ended character. (p. 84)

Thinking-centered lessons are often described as "constructivist learning" in current progressive education literature. Though there is an academic debate over the proper understanding of "educational constructivism" (Fosnot, 1996), the term generally refers to educational activities that invite students to make personal sense of subject matter—to ***construct*** meaning—by drawing connections between their pertinent past experiences and the content they are studying (Brooks and

Brooks, 1993; Henderson, 1996). If this content is not, in some way, relevant to students' lives, active constructions of meaning will not occur. Students can be forced to memorize material and to engage in repeated drill activities, but they can't be forced to think for themselves. Constructivist learning is, therefore, invitational in nature and requires a teacher's best facilitative artistry. Teachers who facilitate constructivist learning are not necessarily opposed to memorization and drill techniques. They may use these methods as part of their facilitative repertoire. However, they don't see these approaches as ends-in-themselves but rather as means to the goal of encouraging students' active meaning making.

An important way to evaluate "thinking-centered" education is through personalized *performance-based outcomes.* When this evaluation approach is used, students are better able to demonstrate the subtle dimensions of their constructivist learning (Herman, Aschbacker, and Winters, 1992). This type of evaluation is not only "personally authentic," it is also "socially authentic" since evaluative judgments in the working world are mostly based on job performances (Allen, 1998). Spady (1994) presents a taxonomy of six increasingly complex ways to think about student learning performances:

1. *Discrete content skills* . . . [such as] spelling specific words, carrying out specific mathematical operations, drawing particular objects, or locating specific features on a map.

2. *Structured task performances* . . . [such as] carrying out a laboratory experiment and comparing its results with established theory; or drawing a map of a region at a specific point in history and contrasting it with a contemporary map of the same region.

3. *Higher order competencies* . . . [such as] analyzing concepts and their interrelations; proposing solutions to multifaceted problems; using complex arrays of data and information to make decisions; planning complex structures, processes, or events; and communicating effectively with public audiences.

4. *Complex unstructured task performances* . . . [such as] . . . defining the parameters, criteria, standards, and modes of execution and evaluation [of a student-created project].

5. *Complex role performances* . . . [where students function as] implementers and performers, . . . problem finders and solvers, . . . planners and designers, . . . creators and producers, . . . learners and thinkers, . . . listeners and communicators, . . . teachers and mentors, . . . supporters and contributors, . . . team members and partners, . . . [and] leaders and organizers.

6. *Life-role functioning* . . . simulated in both typical educational settings and in the real-world contexts with which schools are connecting more and more through business partnerships and service learning programs. (pp. 20–22)

Spady (1994) notes that movement up this taxonomy requires increasing professional flexibility in terms of both how learning performances are conceptualized and how they are evaluated.

Students' Self-Learning

Teaching for democratic living fosters a certain type of *self*-learning. Teachers can help their students see themselves as active lifelong learners. This type of self-learning incorporates a wide range of personal capacities. In the classic 1962 yearbook of the Association for Supervision and Curriculum Development (ASCD), entitled *Perceiving, Behaving, Becoming: A New Focus for Education,* Earl Kelley, Carl Rogers, A. H. Maslow, and Arthur Combs set out their views on the nature and development of the healthy self, which they characterize as the "self-actualizing" individual (Combs, 1962). This type of person is engaged in a process of continuous "becoming" (Maslow, 1962) through active, multifaceted transactions with the world in which he or she is immersed. As Kelley (1962) notes, caring and mutually respectful social relations are essential for this self-learning. Particularly when we are young and vulnerable, our parents' and/or significant others' perceptions of our capacities to grow—communicated through direct and indirect messages—can have an enormous impact on our sense of ourselves as "becoming" beings.

Greene (1978) aptly characterizes this self-learning as a process of "wide-awakeness." We increasingly become more cognitively, emotionally, physically, aesthetically, and spiritually

attuned to ourselves and others. We learn to activate our imaginations, to welcome new insights, and to change our minds as circumstances warrant. As we begin to see ourselves as people who
are engaged in a lifelong journey of inquiry growth, we are willing to refine our beliefs through reciprocal dialogue with diverse
others. We actively support the emergence of growth-oriented
"public spaces" (Greene, 1988), such as schools, churches, community organizations, and television talk shows, where participants celebrate the broadening of their horizons through an interplay of different perspectives.

This self-learning stresses social-emotional growth. Goleman (1995) argues that a person's emotional intelligence is a
more significant factor in life success than a person's IQ. He
summarizes his studies of emotional intelligence as "knowing
what your feelings are and using your feelings to make good decisions in life" (O'Neil, 1996, p. 6). Social-emotional growth is
fostered in caring and supportive learning environments that invite active student participation in classroom and school management activities. Students are asked to work on their conflict
resolution skills, and they participate in peer mediation activities. The school is viewed as a caring community of lifelong
learners, and students are taught to become active and responsible members of this community. Schneider (1996) writes: "If
we want to nurture students who will grow into lifelong learners, into self-directed seekers, into the kind of adults who are
morally responsible even when someone is not looking, then
we need to give them opportunities to practice making choices
and reflecting on the outcomes" (p. 26).

This self-learning places a high value on the development of
each student's unique gifts, what Armstrong (1998) characterizes
as a student's "genius." He explains:

> Every student is a genius. I do not mean this in the psychome-
> tric sense of the word, in which an individual must score above
> the upper 99th percentile on a standardized measure of intelli-
> gence to qualify. . . . For the meaning of *genius* used here, I
> have gone back to the origins of the word itself. . . . The word
> *genius* derives from Greek and Latin words meaning "to
> beget," "to be born," or "to come into being" (it is closely re-
> lated to the word *genesis*). . . . The genius is a symbol for an
> individual's potential: all that a person may be that lies locked

inside during the early years of development. So, when we say as educators that we want to help students to develop their potential, we're essentially saying that we want to assist them in finding their inner genius and support them in guiding it into pathways that can lead to personal fulfillment and to the benefit of those around them. (pp.1–2)

Armstrong (1998) then notes that this type of self-learning requires a classroom environment guided by five principles: "(1) freedom to choose, (2) open-ended exploration, (3) freedom from judgment, (4) honoring of every student's experience, and (5) belief in every student's genius" (p. 60).

Students' Social Learning

Teaching for democratic living fosters a certain type of *social* learning. Democratic educators help their students think about *equity, diversity,* and *civility issues.* They want their students to cultivate the dispositions of critically informed citizens who are respectful of the democratic traditions and ideals of their pluralistic society.

Equity issues address fundamental questions of fairness and justice, particularly with reference to class, race, gender, and sexual orientation diversity. Educational programs that foster a critical awareness of equity issues possess several key characteristics. Critical reasoning must begin at an early age; students must be challenged to confront basic cultural stereotypes; and grading policies must send encouraging messages to all students. The teaching staff should be culturally diverse and should model equitable social relations. And parallel to the preceding curriculum discussion on learning to think of oneself as a lifelong learner, schools should be relatively small; and classes should emphasize collaborative working relationships.

Matthews, Binkley, Crisp, and Gregg (1997/1998) discuss an elementary sex equity project, in which fifth graders are challenged to confront their gender biases. In this year-long program, students are first sensitized to gender equity issues by discussing brief dramatizations of fair and unfair classroom interactions on a CD-ROM: "For example, one scene shows boys and girls looking through a microscope. Boys have the equipment. When a girl asks to see, a boy replies that science is for boys. When that same scene is replayed—with shared equipment—a girl says to the group, 'Look what I found,' and a boy in the group says, 'Science is cool' " (p. 55). The fifth-grade students are next asked to read and discuss fictional cases that address gender equity issues. This case study inquiry learning led to several positive outcomes, including some student advice for teachers: " 'When you're calling on people, call on a girl, then a boy, then a girl, then a boy next.' Or, 'call on everybody, even the ones not raising their hand.' Another student suggested, 'A way you can be fair to both boys and girls is to always have an open mind. Don't let just the girls run errands and don't let just boys run errands' " (Matthews et al., 1997/1998, p. 57).

Educating for *diversity* should focus on the awareness, acceptance, and appreciation of human differences—with a sensitivity to democratic traditions and ideals. James Banks, who is arguably the most important scholar on educating for diversity in the United States today, states in a recent interview: "Our critics misinterpret multiculturalism by claiming we are cultural relativists. Nowhere in my writing, or in the writing of other multicultural educators, do we advocate cultural relativism. Rather, we make a strong, unequivocal commitment to democracy, to basic American values of justice and equality" (Brandt, 1994, p. 31). It is Banks' point that multicultural education is closely linked to principles of equity and to democratic ideals (Banks, 1994).

To illustrate good multicultural education, Wass Van Ausdall (1994) describes how she teaches an elementary school class that mirrors "the diversity of ethnic groups and nationalities in our society . . ." (p. 32). Students read and discuss literature from diverse cultures around the planet. They undertake collaborative learning projects that focus on civil rights abuses: "One group of students prepared a presentation in which Dr. Manette's 18-year secret imprisonment was compared to the disappearance of children in Argentina and their mothers' protest march in the town square" (Wass Van Ausdall, 1994, p. 33). Students are also asked to keep daily journals on their multicultural educational learning. These journals are used to assist private and sensitive teacher-student communications. Any public sharing of journal entries during classroom discussions is at the discretion of each student.

Educating for *civility* is closely related to educating for *equity* and *diversity.* The focus of these programs is on helping students understand that the right to dissent in a pluralistic society with democratic ideals "stands on a commitment to listening to those who disagree with us" (Scherer, 1997, p. 5). There are several key curricular features of educational programs that are designed to foster civility. Students are taught to appreciate the complexity of many social issues and that many highly contested topics, such as government policy on abortion, are not properly understood through simplistic either/or thinking or through demonizing those who have opposing points of view. This type of sophisticated social inquiry requires modeling of, and experience with, civil discourse. Parker (1997) presents several examples of this social learning approach:

§ Children are gathered on the rug to deliberate a proposed rule that would forbid a child from telling other children that they cannot join in a game.

§ High school juniors are weighing the possible causes of the witchcraft accusations in Salem in order to decide on the most probable cause.

§ Students are assigned to cooperative "jigsaw" teams to create a museum exhibit on the Salem witchcraft phenomenon. (p. 21)

There is ample research evidence that community service learning assists this type of social education and helps students think of themselves as active citizens (Boyte and Skelton, 1997). Service learning programs can involve students in a variety of valuable projects: from cleaning up neighborhoods to helping non-profit voluntary organizations.

CRAFT REFLECTION

Teaching for subject matter, self, and social learning is technically sophisticated. It involves a lot of knowledge about appropriate techniques, strategies, and methods. This is the craft side of education (Tom, 1984), and it is essential to the teaching artistry focus of this book. Huebner (1962/1999) notes that all forms of human artistry involve the challenge of refining one's

know-how. He writes that artists must possess "consummate skill"; they must be "masters" of their medium (p. 32):

> As the writer shapes words to his meanings, so the sculptor shapes clay of stone, the painter pigment, and the composer sounds. Not simply a matter of physical control over the instruments of the craft, the brush, typewriter, chisel, piano; the artist has cognitive control over the media, knowing immediately and almost intuitively the possibilities of various stones, the blending and glazing characteristics of the pigments, and the harmonious qualities of the strings. Furthermore he [sic] is a master of the abstract knowledge about the craft: metrics, plot and character development, perspective, balance, melody, counterpoint, and other aspects of the lore and science of the craft. (p. 33)

Just as writers, sculptors, painters, and composers must develop their craft, so must teachers. Throughout their careers, they must continually refine their skills in the general areas of program designing, lesson planning, and classroom management. They must become highly skilled problem solvers while engaged in complex teaching-learning activities. In other words, they must become masters of their particular classroom domain.

Cultivating the craft dimensions of one's teaching is a highly personal matter requiring much dedicated effort. Each teacher must engage in recurring cycles of ***instructional study, application, observation,*** and ***reflection,*** as depicted in Figure 1.2. Teachers must continuously study new ways to work with their students, decide how to apply their studies to their particular circumstances, observe the results of their applications, and then reflect on their observations. Teachers maximize their "experiential learning" (Kolb, 1984) when their reflections are guided by the following questions:

- Is this new craft knowledge useful?
- Should I retain this knowledge or discard it?
- Do I need to further refine this new knowledge?
- If so, how should I proceed? What new applications should I make?
- On what basis am I making these decisions? What are the criteria for my craft decisions?

Figure 1.2

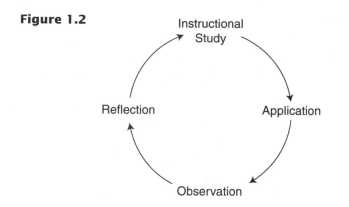

These five questions are consistent with Dewey's (1910/1933) understanding of good reflective practice. Dewey argues that thoughtful practitioners consider both the underlying premises and the consequences of their instructional actions.

The preceding five questions provide a scaffolding—a set of guiding questions—for craft reflection. ***Craft reflection is defined as a teacher's thinking during recurring cycles of instructional study, application, observation, and reflection.*** A teacher's craft reflections occur in a context of continuous study on the "how-tos" of teaching. If a teacher does not continuously study new instructional approaches, if there is no personal application of these studies in the classroom, and if there is no careful observation of the consequences of these applications, then the teacher is not practicing craft reflection. A teacher with twenty-three years of experience was asked to provide a concise overview of her craft reflections.* Here is what she wrote.

I have been a music teacher for twenty years. From the beginning to date, I have had a vision and a desire to give all that I could to the children in my care. What a ride it has been! Writing this narrative has been an opportunity for me to view my growth through an interesting lens; one that has been both reflective and enlightening.

---

*Contributed by Jan Wolf.

Thinking back over my years in education, it has been interesting for me to see the manner in which I have evolved as a teacher. I remember those undergraduate methods classes. We were involved in a lot of peer teaching, class discussion, and field experience. Our textbooks were written in a general manner with broad overviews regarding teaching techniques. Planning for peer teaching relied on personal creativity and popular vocal music textbooks that were in our library. Class discussions related to assigned reading, field experiences, and peer teaching critiques. We wrote lesson plans for imaginary children and immersed ourselves in writing papers regarding educational theory, research, and methods. At the completion of my undergraduate work, I felt I was ready to teach. Graduation was a wonderful moment! Even more exciting was getting a job!

My first public school position was working musically with suburban children in grades K–3. I enjoyed young children and was pleased with this assignment. I felt my university coursework had prepared me well. I knew how to make lesson plans, teach a song, and had a thorough knowledge of research, theory, and methods. As the first day approached, I began to get cold feet. I was at a loss as to how to begin. What should I do on the first day of class? On my desk were the music textbooks as well as the curriculum guide for the district. I knew I was to combine the aesthetic sense of music with its theoretical aspect. But the question of how to start went over and over in my mind. Sensing my ambivalence, a veteran teacher stepped forward with advice. "Begin at the beginning," she said. "Page one, song one." And so I did. It worked for awhile until the frustration set in.

The children were seated in desks in a row. The textbooks were relatively new and full of age-appropriate materials. The recorded music packaged with the textbook provided clear and pleasant listening. Why was I frustrated? Why did the children seem bored? Why was I spending so much time on discipline problems? I began to seriously consider finding answers to these questions. I found that one question led to another and another and another. Now I had generated a mental list of questions. I observed the children, noted their reactions, and wondered what was going wrong. What did I need to do to create a joyful, positive aura in my classroom? What techniques should I be using that would alleviate the discipline problems and boredom?

As I reflected on my questions and observations, it seemed to me that I needed to better support the learning of the children in order to dismiss behavior problems and get rid of the boredom. I needed to find a way to engage them. I knew I had several sources of help for my dilemma. First, I made plans to attend the annual state conference for music educators. As an undergraduate, we had been encouraged to attend and my experience told me that I would find some answers there. That was a few months away; I had to do something now. To start, I turned to colleagues and professional reading. Conversations with other music teachers gave me a new picture of possibilities. Time spent observing a wonderful music teacher in another building proved worthwhile. I pulled the *Music Educators Journal* out from under my stack of magazines and discovered articles appropriate to solving my dilemma. February came and I attended the state music educators' conference. This conference provided a great deal of enlightenment. Listening to and learning from master teachers and authorities in the field was extremely helpful.

As the year continued and then moved on to two and three, I found my technique beginning to evolve. I was learning to trust the advice of colleagues, acquire knowledge from the literature, and follow my own intuition. I was intent on providing the children the best music education background that could be developed. It was a matter of following the cycle of instructional study, application, observation, and reflection that guided me through this process. The self-questioning never stopped. Without that, I would have become stagnant.

As the years wore on, I found myself becoming more and more innovative in my technique. No more "page one, song one" for me! I now looked at the music textbooks as supplements to my well-researched repertoire. The desks in a row, so neatly arranged by the custodian, were stacked in the corner of the room. I replaced them with colorful tape marking off circles on the floor. I invited the children to sit there during class. We played singing games, acquired a great repertoire of songs, and learned theory through playing instruments. Paper/pencil, textbook-driven activities and desks in a row were no longer part of my teaching day.

When I transferred to the kindergarten building, I struggled for awhile with technique, methods, and materials. The textbook was always on my desk and I had returned to the packaged repertoire. Once more, I was frustrated. The children weren't responding well, as evidenced by behavior problems and lack of attention. Again, I turned to colleagues, the literature, professional associations, and university coursework for my remedies. It worked as it had done before! I found a methodology I liked through professional reading. I attended a

week-long workshop during the summer to prepare for u
gram with the kindergarten children. It was like beginning
The next year was wonderful! I attribute the joy to my on
tioning and continual search for answers. I was freed from
books, recorded music, and structured teaching. The staff, pa
the children especially responded in such a positive manner. W
lished "All-School Sings" and invited parents to join us. Every o
the repertoire; it was familiar and pleasant. I knew I was meet
trict curriculum standards through involving children in musical
ties that would serve as foundational skills for their later study.

My days in the classroom are far from over. I am still working
young children. I have not stopped questioning and never will. I cont
to attend conferences, read profusely, take university coursework,
collaborate with colleagues. I have come a long way from those und
graduate methods days. I have evolved through ongoing inquiry. It ha
led me toward fulfilling my desire to give children the best.

PROFESSIONAL ARTISTRY THROUGH INQUIRY

If an educator is only interested in teaching subject matter well, then ***craft reflection*** will probably be sufficient for his or her professional growth. Such an educator can function as a good technician, as someone who has refined skillful ways to teach a particular subject at a basic and/or an advanced level. His or her skills might even be sufficiently polished to be characterized as "artistic" in a limited, technical sense of this term. Though such professionals deserve respect, particularly if they have worked hard to develop their craft, they are not the focus of this book for a very important reason. ***Though they are effective subject matter instructors, they have not developed their ability to teach for democratic living.*** Their "capacity building" (Darling-Hammond, 1997) has been limited to the ***know-how*** of their vocation—to the craft side of their profession. They are, in effect, well-trained technicians. If you know such teachers, then you undoubtedly understand the strengths and limitations of their professional development.

To teach for democratic living requires the integration of five forms of inquiry into your ongoing craft reflections. In this book, we will call this the challenge of ***professional artistry through inquiry.*** These five forms of professional study are: *public moral inquiry, multiperspective inquiry, deliberative inquiry, autobiographical inquiry,* and *critical inquiry.* When you regularly practice these forms of inquiry, you are developing your capacities to teach for democratic living.

Through *public moral inquiry,* you consider the ethics, mores, values, and virtues of democracy as a way of living. The discussion of the three "basics" of democratic living in this chapter is, essentially, a manifestation of public moral inquiry. In chapter 2, you will be introduced to a scaffolding (again, a set of guiding questions) for public moral inquiry. If you apply this scaffolding to your practice, you might construct a different set of democratic fundamentals. You are encouraged to think imaginatively and to reach your own conclusions. The fact that people think in divergent ways is an important feature of disciplined human inquiry.

Through *multiperspective inquiry,* which is the topic of chapter 3, you explore diverse perspectives on the democracy and education relationship. There is much to consider when teaching for democratic living, as illustrated in the previous **3S** student learning discussion. When you strive to facilitate your students' direct ***experiences*** with society's democratic ideals, you must approach curriculum and teaching as an "extraordinarily complicated conversation" (Pinar, Reynolds, Slattery, and Taubman, 1995, p. 848). However, you will not be able to participate in a sophisticated educational conversation unless you broaden your professional horizons through clarifying your personal beliefs.

Through *deliberative inquiry,* which is the topic of chapter 4, you develop your ability to respond to your students' learning problems in creative and personally caring ways. As Eisner (1994) notes, imaginative and sensitive deliberation lies at the heart of teaching artistry:

> Teaching can be done as badly as anything else. It can be wooden, mechanical, mindless, and wholly unimaginative. But when it is sensitive, intelligent, and creative—those qualities that confer upon it the status of an art—it should, in my view, not be regarded, as it so often is by some, as an expression of unfathomable talent or luck but as an example of humans exercising the highest levels of their intelligence. (p. 156)

The 3S's of teaching for democratic learning require this so-phisticated type of professional intelligence.

Through *autobiographical inquiry,* which is the topic of chapter 5, you examine teaching as a personal calling to a caring vocation. You think about how you can construct your own unique "voice-from-the-heart" by becoming attuned to the aesthetic and spiritual dimensions of your daily work. Aoki (1992) captures the essence of autobiographical inquiry:

> All of these scientific and technical understandings of teaching emerge from our interest in intellectual and manipulative grasp and control. But in so understanding, we must be attuned to the fact that while those understandings that can be grasped are uncannily correct, the essence of teaching still eludes our grasp. What we need to do is to break away from the attitude of grasping and seek to be more properly oriented to what teaching is, so we can attune ourselves to the call of what teaching is. (p. 20)

To teach for democratic living requires educators to contemplate the heart-felt "call" of their profession.

Through *critical inquiry,* which is the topic of chapter 6, you cultivate your awareness of social, economic, and political inequities. Teaching for democratic living requires a careful reconsideration of the overt, tacit, and covert power relations between people. When *critical inquiry* is integrated into teachers' reflective practices, it is often called *praxis.* Beyer and Apple (1988) explain:

> The literature [in the curriculum and teaching field] bounds with material on the "reflective practitioner," and some of it is very good. However, we wish to go further. Our objective is perhaps best embodied in the concept of *praxis.* This involves not only the justifiable concern for reflective action, but thought and action combined and enlivened by a sense of power and politics. It involves both conscious understanding of and action in schools on solving our daily problems. These problems will not go away by themselves, after all. But it also requires critically reflective practices that alter the material and ideological conditions that cause the problems we are facing as educators in the first place. (p. 4, emphasis in original)

The relationship between craft reflection and these five forms of inquiry is depicted in Figure 1.3. Notice how each form of inquiry overlaps with the experiential learning cycle of craft reflection. This schematic also conveys the idea that ***professional artistry,*** as described in this book, is a matter of degree. Craft reflection and all five forms of inquiry are equally important in a teacher's journey to professional artistry. The Figure 1.3 image is shown early in chapters 2 through 6, and you will notice that the particular form of inquiry under consideration is shaded.

To assist your studies, chapters 2–6 are organized in an identical format. Each chapter opens with a vignette that provides a snapshot of a teacher practicing the form of inquiry

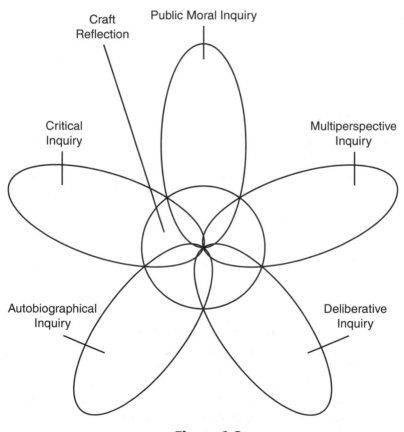

Figure 1.3

being examined. The form of inquiry is then introduced and explained. Next, a scaffolding for that form of inquiry is presented in a bulleted format. It is important that this scaffolding *not* be treated as a tightly sequenced set of technical steps. Though craft reflection can, at times, be handled in this way, this is not the case for professional inquiry. The scaffolding should be treated as a set of potentially helpful questions. The degree to which they assist your inquiries, they should be used; the degree to which they inhibit your inquiries, they should be discarded. Finally, the chapter ends with a narrative written by an experienced teacher who has integrated the chapter's form of inquiry into her craft reflections.

Though each professional account is personally and contextually unique, the stories share three characteristics. The narratives are composed by highly dedicated teachers who think in terms of their interactions with students. They discuss their inquiries in the context of their interactions with their students. All the teacher narratives are autobiographical in style. Teacher inquiry is a highly personal matter, involving unique features of each educator's personality. Finally, the inquiry accounts are more subtle and diffuse than the theoretical discussions and the scaffoldings that precede them. This difference has a simple explanation. Though five distinctive forms of inquiry have been analytically identified and dissected for the study purposes of this book, teachers' actual inquiries are not so neatly categorized. Educational inquiry is a very complex, idiosyncratic, and holistic process (Connelly and Clandinin, 1988; Short, 1991); no one element of a teacher's thinking can be neatly isolated from any other element. For example, it is not possible to precisely demarcate where public moral inquiry ends and multiperspective inquiry begins. When we practice these two forms of inquiry, they become intermingled in our thoughts. Figure 1.3 has been designed, in part, to demonstrate the interrelated nature of the five forms of teacher inquiry in this text.

This book is organized around a particular inquiry sequence. *Public moral inquiry* helps educators think about the "big picture" of their professional commitments. What vision of virtuous living guides all their efforts? Through *multiperspective inquiry*, teachers explore the complexities of the democracy and education relationship; through *deliberative inquiry*, teachers cultivate their capacity to respond creatively and caringly to these complexities. *Autobiographical inquiry* helps teachers become attuned to the aesthetic and spiritual dimensions of their professional calling. Through *critical inquiry,* teachers' investigations come "full circle" as they explore the ethical and political implications of their moral visions. What are the emancipatory possibilities and constraints of *teaching for democratic living?*

The final chapter of this book, chapter 7, addresses the topic of *transformative teacher leadership.* There is a reason for ending the text on this subject. Because teaching for democratic living is such a challenging undertaking, teachers will find it difficult to strive for this professional standard by themselves. They need to find ways to support each other's continuing study efforts, and they need to work with supportive administrators to transform schools into inquiry learning communities. Transformative teacher leaders are educators who are deeply committed to their own professional development journey, eagerly participate in collaborative study activities with colleagues, and willingly assume school reform responsibilities. They understand the value of collegial inquiry for teachers, for schools, and for society as a whole.

CONCLUSION

This book presents a very challenging *inquiry* standard for teachers for a very important reason. *Democracy not only demands constitutionally guaranteed political and legal institutions, it requires the dedicated services of public educators.* Without such professionals, societies with democratic ideals cannot reach their full potential.

Hopefully, you are reading this book as a future or current teacher who is already committed to a professional life of continuous, disciplined study. You already believe that teachers should develop their inquiry capacities, and you look forward to your own journey of professional artistry. Perhaps, however, you are at a point where you feel that the best you can do is practice your ongoing craft reflections. You have neither the time nor the energy to cultivate a sophisticated inquiry repertoire. Working on the technical side of your job is about all you can handle. You are simply too busy. Such feelings are common for teachers during the first three to five years of their careers. If you feel this way, there is still value in studying this book. You may reach a point in your career when you can begin to *teach for democratic living.*

Throughout the venerable history of education, there have always been teachers who have been more than subject matter specialists (Broudy and Palmer, 1965). If they could achieve such professional excellence, why can't you? Transforming one's chosen craft into a form of artistry is an age-old human problem. In this book, you are being asked to think about this problem from the perspective of democracy and education. You are being introduced to a high standard of continuing professional study. Welcome to the challenges of *professional artistry through inquiry.* Welcome to the noble calling and the exciting venture of becoming a teacher for democratic living.

The experienced teacher, who earlier provided a brief overview of her craft reflections, has also composed a welcoming statement for this book. She has written a very personal narrative on why she feels teachers should cultivate their professional artistry through a life of inquiry.

Teacher Narrative*

If you are reading this book, you are probably about to embark on your teaching career or are currently in its early years. Congratulations! Teaching is a noble profession. It is one that affects children, parents, and community in ways that we may never know personally. Ours is a career choice that involves dedication, love, and enthusiasm for the subject matter we teach, as well as the children in our care.

The field of education is filled with teachers representing a mixture of philosophies and standards. Each is informed through his or her own personal background and experience. Some take comfort in

---

*Contributed by Jan Wolf.

knowing that a principal or supervisor will direct their thinking. They have a better sense of doing the right thing, knowing they are conforming to district policy and rules. Others have a broader sense of knowing but are caught in a nightmare of policy and procedure, wishing to move away from it but not knowing how. They struggle daily as they try to serve two masters. Still others begin with a vision of what is good and right for children. They move forward with compliance to policy but are independent thinkers in terms of implementation and practice. These are the movers and shakers in the field of educational thinking today! These are transformative thinkers. It is this latter group that this book is all about. Transformative thinkers have an understanding of the five forms of professional study featured in this text: public moral inquiry, multiperspective inquiry, deliberative inquiry, autobiographical inquiry, and critical inquiry. My personal lifestyle and educational background have given me the privilege of understanding transformative thinking. It has not always been an easy road, but it has been personally satisfying. It has allowed me to be true to myself.

When you go out into the teaching world, you will come upon influences and be forced to make professional choices. It can be difficult to think independently in the throes of a veteran teacher who influences through intimidation. These are teachers who are informed through their motto: "But we've always done it this way." They can shake a person's independence if it is not built on a solid foundation. Other teachers question procedure but are ambivalent about implementing change. These are teachers who abide by the motto: "I wish it could be different." They are frequently desirous of rethinking and restructuring but lack the tools to do so. They can seem confused to a person armed with tools to think. Still other teachers are always on the cutting edge. They are collaborative thinkers who are informed through theory and research. Their motto is: "Anything is possible." They have a vision of what is good for children. They proceed with confidence and sometimes appear to be wearing buffers and blinders as they challenge the veteran teachers and try to encourage those in limbo. They attend conferences, have a stack of professional reading on their desks, appreciate the value of continuing university coursework, view children as capable, see parents as part of the team, and constantly make efforts to personally evolve. They are the teachers who have accepted the challenge of professional artistry through a life of inquiry.

When I look at my own life, I see teaching as a career choice from very early on. The educational influences in my personal surroundings were strong and positive and made a powerful impact on me. My parents were both teachers. Conversations in our home frequently revolved around faculty, students, and school activities as my mother and father discussed their work environment. My own education included an enlightened teacher as early as second grade. Mrs. Hoffman did everything through project work. The word "test" was not a part of her vocabulary and yet we all learned and learned in depth. Involvement in teaching Bible School, working on a playground, serving as a camp counselor, and membership in Future Teachers of America in high school, along with my parent's influence, all had their place in forming my educational vision and ideals.

Perhaps the greatest influence on my teaching came from my father. As a high school teacher, he shaped the lives of many students in his wood shop. Today, we would classify his area of expertise as technology. He had a reputation districtwide for strict discipline, quality work, and innovative curriculum. His classes were filled with boys who were in the nonacademic track. However, unlike a lot of wood shop classes, my father's students created desks, bedroom suites, and other furniture for their homes. It was not unusual for a student to rent a truck to carry his project home.

My father was a transformative thinker long before the term was created. He was constantly using his observational skills to reflect on instruction and application. His reflection then led to change. He used inquiry to determine need, policy, and procedure. For example, he went beyond the traditional boundaries of curriculum by establishing a wood shop class for girls. This was unheard of at the time. Several girls approached him about the possibility. He gave it thought and then pushed to have it included in the curriculum. He won! He taught the girls to handle tools, make simple repairs, and create wonderful wooden pieces for their homes and families. He also established a wood shop class for the academic track students. My father felt that eliminating honor students from his classes was an injustice! He worked through the bureaucracy of the school district to develop and implement this innovative class.

At the time, of course, I took all of his educational vitality for granted. Conversations at home told me that he was moving ahead of traditional policy. I could tell that he had not taken the easy road, but I knew that his willingness and ability to rock the boat became the bonus for the students. The gratitude of the students and their parents, as well as his reputation for educational leadership in his field, is still part of his legacy. He is remembered for his educational standards and innovative ideas. I have long admired his courage.

My first personal reality check in education came in my student teaching. It was there that I began to realize that I was on a different thinking track than a lot of people. I was assigned to a third-grade class in a suburban school. I remember riding with a group of friends who were also student teaching, and I recall the animated conversations we had about our personal experiences as we traveled to and from our assignments.

My school utilized a textbook-driven curriculum. My cooperating teacher was a wonderful person, but she complied exactly with dictated policy and procedure. Of course, as a student teacher, I took her lead. She was compassionate and understanding, and we both loved the group of twenty-five eight-year-olds in our charge. As the weeks wore on, however, I began to wonder about the children and their thinking. My role in this class was director instead of facilitator of learning. I was not comfortable with that. It seemed to me that these children lacked involvement and responsibility for their own learning, which might be a detriment to their ability to think and reason. I was beginning to question.

The organization of learning in that school became an obstacle for me. I wanted more for the children. I felt uncomfortable with my role in their learning. I knew the children had ideas, thoughts, and interests. The questions were accumulating in my mind. Could there be another way to teach? As a student teacher, I was not afforded the opportunity to make change. However, when I became employed as a teacher, all of that shifted. From my first job through my current position, I have always had an educational vision and have questioned, questioned, questioned. One of the most enlightened principals in my career defined my projects as pilot programs. He loved my transformative thinking. Justifying my curriculum changes in that manner avoided the bureaucracy and allowed for instant implementation.

My questioning has been ongoing, and my inquiry has never stopped. Throughout these twenty-some years in the field of education, my depth of understanding has changed and grown. I have come to realize that teaching, for me, is a calling. I have learned that obstacles can be viewed as barriers or hurdles. Remaining open to change with willingness, sense of courage, and informed sense of being has allowed me to challenge my own thinking, as well as the thinking of others. Attending workshops, keeping abreast of current trends, and reflecting on my instructional practice have been and are a part of my personal design.

As I look over this text, I only wish something like this had been available to me as I embarked on my career. Fortunately, I experienced my father's positive role modeling and professional courage. Through his cycle of inquiry, innovation, and implementation, I learned that creating change could be a good thing. He showed me a sense of direction and ability to be analytical and reflective. I have used that plus my intuitive tools. Although I often found myself in disagreement with colleagues, I forged ahead anyway. The results were well worth the frustrations.

I found enlightened teachers within the boundaries of each teaching assignment. In fact, I think we found each other! We collaborated, inquired, reflected, and implemented educational ideas, always with a vision of what was best for the children. Our enthusiasm often caught the attention of teachers stuck in a rut or unable to find a path to change. It was wonderful to see them move away from the past.

I challenge you to view your frustrations as hurdles rather than obstacles! Keep in mind that obstacles will stop you but hurdles move you forward! Tools to do so are within the bindings of this book. Consider what you read carefully. In our hands, as teachers, are the lives of many children. It is essential that we support their learning in the most informed way we can. With this text, you will find yourself among the elite of educators: those who accept the challenge of professional artistry through inquiry.

REFERENCES

Allen, D. (Ed.). (1998). *Assessing student learning: From grading to understanding*. New York: Teachers College Press.

Aoki, T. T. (1992). Layered voices of teaching: The uncannily correct and the elusively true. In W. F. Pinar & W. M. Reynolds (Eds.), *Understanding curriculum as phenomenological and deconstructed text* (pp. 17–27). New York: Teachers College Press.

Armstrong, T. (1998). *Awakening genius in the classroom.* Alexandria, VA: Association for Supervision and Curriculum Development.

Banks, J. A. (1994). Transforming the mainstream curriculum. *Educational Leadership, 51* (8), 4–8.

Beyer, L. E., & Apple, M. W. (1988). Values and politics in the curriculum. In L. E. Beyer & M. W. Apple (Eds.), *The curriculum: Problems, politics, and possibilities* (pp. 3–16). Albany, NY: State University of New York Press.

Boyte, H. C., & Skelton, N. (1997). The legacy of public work. *Educational Leadership, 54* (5), 12–17.

Brandt, R. (1994). On educating for diversity: A conversation with James A. Banks. *Educational Leadership, 51* (8), 28–31.

Brooks, J. G., & Brooks, M. G. (1993). *In search of understanding: The case for constructivist classrooms.* Alexandria, VA: Association for Supervision and Curriculum Development.

Broudy, H. S., & Palmer, J. K. (1965). *Exemplars of teaching method.* Chicago: Rand McNally.

Combs, A. W. (Chair). (1962). *Perceiving, behaving, becoming: A new focus for education.* Washington, DC: Association for Supervision and Curriculum Development.

Connelly, F. M., & Clandinin, D. J. (1988). *Teachers as curriculum planners: Narrative of experience.* New York: Teachers College Press.

Darling-Hammond, L. (1997). Reframing the school reform agenda: Developing capacity for school transformation. In E. Clinchy (Ed.), *Transforming public education: A new course for America's future* (pp. 38–55). New York: Teachers College Press.

Dewey, J. (1933). *How we think: A restatement of the relation of reflective thinking to the educative process* (2nd ed.). Boston: Heath. (Original work published 1910)

Dewey, J. (1936). The social significance of academic freedom. *The Social Frontier, 2* (6), 165–166.

Dewey, J. (1985). Ethics. In J. A. Boydston (Ed.), *The later works of John Dewey, 1925–1953* (Vol. 7). Carbondale, IL: Southern Illinois University Press. (Original work published 1932)

Eisner, E. W. (1994). *The educational imagination: On the design and evaluation of school programs* (3rd ed.). New York: Macmillan.

Fosnot, C. T. (Ed.). (1996). *Constructivism: Theory, perspectives, and practice.* New York: Teachers College Press.

Garrison, J. (1997). *Dewey and eros: Wisdom and desire in the art of teaching.* New York: Teachers College Press.

Goleman, D. (1995). *Emotional intelligence: Why it can matter more than IQ.* New York: Bantam Books.

Greene, M. (1978). *Landscapes of learning.* New York: Teachers College Press.

Greene, M. (1988). *The dialectic of freedom.* New York: Teachers College Press.

Henderson, J. G. (1996). *Reflective teaching: The study of your constructivist practices* (2nd ed.). Upper Saddle River, NJ: Merrill/Prentice Hall.

Herman, J. L., Aschbacker, R. R., & Winters, L. (1992). *A practical guide to alternative assessment.* Alexandria, VA: Association for Supervision and Curriculum Development.

Huebner, D. E. (1999). The art of teaching. In V. Hillis (Ed.), *The lure of the transcendent: Collected essays by Dwayne E. Huebner* (pp. 23–35). Mahwah, NJ: Erlbaum. (Original work published 1962)

Kelley, E. C. (1962). The fully functioning self. In A. W. Combs (Chair), *Perceiving, behaving, becoming: A new focus for education* (pp. 9–20). Washington, DC: Association for Supervision and Curriculum Development.

Kolb, D. A. (1984). *Experiential learning: Experience as the source of learning and development.* Upper Saddle River, NJ: PTR Prentice Hall.

Maslow, A. H. (1962). Some basic propositions of a growth and self-actualization psychology. In A. W. Combs (Chair), *Perceiving, behaving, becoming: A new focus for education* (pp. 34–49). Washington, DC: Association for Supervision and Curriculum Development.

Matthews, C. E., Binkley, W., Crisp, A., & Gregg, K. (1997/1998). Challenging gender bias in fifth grade. *Educational Leadership, 55* (4), 54–57.

Meier, D. (1997). Habits of mind: Democratic values and the creation of effective learning communities. In B. S. Kogan (Ed.), *Common schools, uncommon futures: A working consensus for school renewal* (pp. 60–73). New York: Teachers College Press.

Noddings, N. (1997). Learning, teaching, and existential meaning. In B. S. Kogan (Ed.), *Common schools, uncommon futures: A working consensus for school renewal* (pp. 49–59). New York: Teachers College Press.

O'Neil, J. (1996). On emotional intelligence: A conversation with Daniel Goleman. *Educational Leadership, 54* (1), 6–11.

Parker, W. C. (1997). The art of deliberation. *Educational Leadership, 54* (5), 18–21.

Perkins, D. (1993/1994). Thinking-centered learning. *Educational Leadership, 51* (4), 84–85.

Pinar, W. F., Reynolds, W. M., Slattery, P., & Taubman, P. M. (1995). *Understanding curriculum: An introduction to the study of historical and contemporary curriculum discourses.* New York: Peter Lang.

Scherer, M. (1997). Perspectives: Zero tolerance in a civil society? *Educational Leadership, 54* (5), 5.

Schneider, E. (1996). Giving students a voice in the classroom. *Educational Leadership, 54* (1), 22–26.

Short, E. C. (1991). Introduction: Understanding curriculum inquiry. In E. C. Short (Ed.), *Forms of curriculum inquiry* (pp. 1–25). Albany, NY: State University of New York Press.

Smith, F. (1990). *To think.* New York: Teachers College Press.

Spady, W. G. (1994). Choosing outcomes of significance. *Educational Leadership, 51* (6), 18–22.

Tom, A. (1984). *Teaching as a moral craft.* New York: Longman.

Wass Van Ausdall, B. (1994). Books offer entry into understanding cultures. *Educational Leadership, 51* (8), 32–35.

CHAPTER 2

PUBLIC MORAL
INQUIRY

❦

Carla Goodall was quite excited as she drove to school Monday morning. She normally listens to the news on the radio as she copes with the morning rush-hour traffic. This time, however, she kept the radio off because she wanted to review for one last time the rationale for her middle school's (grades 5–7) new "Let's Get Connected" program. Carla had assumed leadership for the design of this program about eighteen months ago in response to three concerns: the increasing number of violent incidents in schools throughout the country, the growing problems of student alienation, and the emergence of divisive social cliques at the school district's junior high school (grades 8–9) and high school (grades 10–12). Carla had chaired a twelve-member curriculum planning team composed of four students (two from the middle school, one from the junior high school, and one from the senior high school), two middle school parents, two representatives from the local Boys' Club and Girls' Club, and four teachers (two middle school teachers, including Carla, one junior high school teacher, and one high school teacher).

The committee's inquiries into how middle school students can feel more connected to their peers in the school, as well as the community at large, had been very far-reaching and visionary. While discussing their views on "moral competency" in a diverse, information-age society, they explored a series of questions. What is the meaning of public morality in our community when we are divided on a number of social issues, including the legality of abortion, gay and lesbian rights, and Internet access? If we can't agree on basic values for living, how can we talk about proper social virtues and character development? On what basis should we feel connected to one another? What draws us together, and what keeps us apart? If the average student in the school district is watching 4—6 hours of television every day with its steady diet of violent programming, how can middle school educators counter such a strong media influence? What public heroes and heroines can teachers ask students to emulate?

There were so many tough questions addressed by the committee that they wondered if they could come up with an educational program that would cultivate a sense of **connection** with others. There were points in their discussions when they all felt despair, but they persisted and were, ultimately, able to design a program. Carla thought back to a major breakthrough moment in the committee's inquiries. At one point in their discussions, they had made a list of pressing social problems in their community, such as the lack of day care support for single-parent mothers, the inadequate nutrition of some of the elderly citizens, and the pollution of the river that ran through downtown. They then translated this list into a set of potential social service projects that could be undertaken by middle school students. After a reporter for the local newspaper highlighted these possible projects in an article, they called an after-school meeting for interested students and their parents. To their amazement, over sixty people attended the meeting! Everyone who came was interested in becoming more connected to their community in one way or another. Conversations were quite passionate, and many heart-warming stories were told. Near the end of this meeting, they began to generate a number of interesting social service projects that could involve middle school students.

This was the impetus Carla's committee needed. Building on that after-school meeting, they were able to create a "Let's Get Connected" program that featured public responsibility and social service. The kick-off event for this program would begin this Monday morning, shortly after Carla arrived at school. It would be a general-assembly activity involving two guest speakers who were locally well known for their community work. Carla had the responsibility of introducing the new program and the two distinguished guests. She hoped she could be inspiring; and as she drove to school, she continued to think about the many uplifting reasons why people should cultivate a sense of connection with one another.

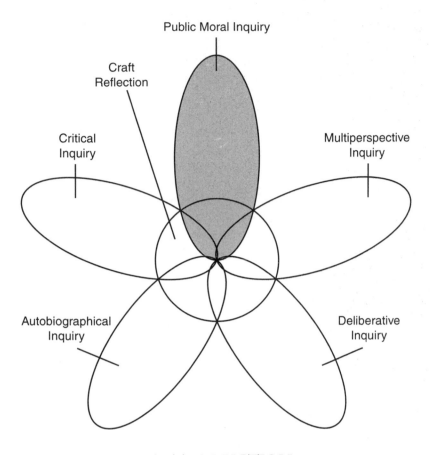

INTRODUCTION

The focus of this chapter is on ***public moral inquiry.*** We begin by examining the meanings of these three terms, individually and then in combination. ***Public*** is defined as those matters that relate to, or affect, people as an organized community or society. Civic concerns, government institutions, and national policies are all part of the ***public*** arena. ***Moral*** refers to principles of right and wrong action and considerations of good and bad character. Morality encompasses concerns about ***ethics, mores, values,*** and ***virtues. Inquiry*** is defined as the act of seeking truth, information, or knowledge about an important matter. ***Inquiry*** refers to open-ended processes of disciplined examination, investigation, and/or research. Because the process is open-ended, those who seek truth, information, or knowledge may not inquire in exactly the same way or come to the same conclusions; and because they are open-minded inquirers, they act from a position of *not-knowing.* They understand that doubt, not true belief, is their constant companion during their inquiries. They know that if they did not tolerate doubts, they could not function as honest, sincere truth-seekers.

Think for a minute about the combination of these three terms. *Public moral inquiry* refers to the disciplined, open-ended examination of what constitutes "good" acts and/or "good" character for *all* people. When teachers engage in *public moral inquiry,* they think about the nature of, and educational support for, virtuous action in their society. Because they are inquiring into questions of *public morality,* they understand that their answers are not final. They see themselves as disciplined students of the "good life" who are always open to additional information, insights, and perspectives.

Teachers who practice *public moral inquiry* also understand the importance of this form of professional investigation. Think for a moment about societies that don't educate for *public morality.* Think about how such societies function. Consider government officials who have no sense of "public duty." They work only to serve themselves, and perhaps their families, friends, or those who give them money. Reflect upon political special-interest groups that have no sense of "public responsibility." Their focus is on their own narrow ideological agenda—their particular true beliefs. Societies that lack a well-developed sense of the "public good" don't function well. In such societies, suspicion pervades daily affairs; virtuous living is mocked; and public heroes or heroines are nonexistent. In contrast, teachers who engage in *public moral inquiry* do so because they want to challenge the cynicism of their era. They want people to reach beyond narrow self-interests—to get in touch with what is noble in their lives. They are inspired by calls to a high-minded life of service to others.

In the next section of this chapter, we first turn to a brief examination of four important *public moral* concerns. Though an entire book could be written on these four considerations, the discussion will be kept relatively brief for two reasons. First, this chapter is actually an extension of chapter 1. As mentioned in the last chapter, the presentation of the three *basic* precepts of democratic living is, actually, a specific manifestation of *public moral inquiry.* After studying this chapter, you, hopefully, will want to pursue your own inquiries into what constitutes a virtuous life in a pluralistic society with democratic ideals. Second, as you also learned in chapter 1, this chapter ends with a narrative written by an experienced, dedicated teacher. Her professional story illustrates the integration of her *public moral inquiries* into her ongoing craft reflections. Because the overall focus of this book is on *those educators who help their students experience democracy as a way of living,* her narrative is particularly important to the text. It not only illustrates a particular public school teacher's *public moral inquiry,* it helps you envision an educator who teaches for democratic living. Because you may never have experienced such a teacher, her story is the longest one in the book.

FOUR PUBLIC MORAL CONCERNS

At least four concerns guide public moral inquiry: (1) *inclusivity,* (2) *constitutionality,* (3) *reciprocity,* and (4) *social philosophy.* These four considerations should not be viewed as the exclusive criteria for "public morality" but rather as vital matters of attention. After studying these four concerns, you may want to add your own "public moral" considerations to this list.

Inclusivity

The principle of *inclusivity* refers to the careful avoidance of in-group and out-group distinctions. The focus of *public moral inquiry* is on *all* citizens of a society—not just some, nor just the majority. Cliquish, tribal, and narrowly ideological positions are rejected. Neither groups nor individuals are marginalized, and no one is turned into an "other." Inquiries are guided by considerations of *social and personal justice.* There is a concern for a "culturally responsive" education that is sensitive to the interplay of values among the school, the home, and the community (Delpit, 1995; Ladson-Billings, 1995).

Though public educators are not well positioned to remedy deeply embedded social structures, policies, and practices that work against select groups of people or individuals, they can still confront social and personal patterns of prejudice. They can challenge racism, sexism, and other forms of bias that surface in their educational settings. They can ensure that their classrooms are relatively bias free. They can raise questions about how their poor, their minority, and their gay and lesbian students are treated. They can promote multicultural education; and, as presented in chapter 1, they can foster social learning that stresses equity, tolerance for diversity, and civility. As a teacher who is concerned about social justice, Kanpol (1994) writes:

> Within the hidden curriculum I will ask myself continually if what I am teaching and constructing is [opposed to deeply embedded patterns of social bias]. . . . I will ask myself in what ways have I empowered the students. Is knowledge presented in authoritarian ways or are students allowed the space to be both critical and transformational about knowledge? I will continually be conscious of the democratic intent of the knowledge I impart and the individuality that I want to foster in class. My hidden agenda is one that aims to challenge existing structures of oppression, alienation, and subordination while simultaneously teaching students the required state-mandated curriculum. In other words, my curriculum is far from objective or innocent. In it lies the cultural politics of knowledge that attempts to challenge students to reformulate their thoughts on self, difference, and other. (p. 156)

Personal justice considerations are closely tied to social justice concerns. However, these two moral considerations should not be confused with one another. Policies that are designed to promote social justice can, in application, be personally unfair to many people. This is an important historical lesson of the twentieth century, clearly demonstrated by the authoritarian and dogmatic practices in the former Soviet Union. Raising questions about personal justice brings the principle of *inclusivity* to the individual level. Teachers who practice inclusivity are careful to teach to *all* students; they are willing to find ways to support each of their student's distinctive approaches to learning. They understand that if a teacher only supports, for example, students who excel in mathematics and the sciences or in athletics, that teacher's work marginalizes certain students. Eisner (1994) writes passionately about the importance of personal equity in education:

> It is possible to afford students opportunities to represent what they have come to know about a subject of study through forms that are congruent with their aptitudes. . . . Such a practice will of course increase the difficulty of making comparisons among the performances of students. But whether the comparative ranking of students is in the long-term best interests of either the students or the society is something that one can certainly argue. In the context of education, the creation of conditions that lead to self-realization is, I believe, a primary aim. If the means through which such realization can occur makes comparative assessments more difficult, so be it. Education is not a horse race. Speed is not the ultimate virtue. What people can become through an educationally caring community is. . . . A broad array of opportunities represented by a wide array of forms of representation and modes of treatment . . . increases educational equity for students by increasing the probability that they will be able to play to their strengths. (pp. 86, 89)

Constitutionality

A "public" is, in part, defined by the relationship between its *ethical* commitments and its *political* associations. The ancient Greeks had a word for this connection. They called an ethical-political association a *polis.* Unfortunately, in modern societies, we often lose sight of the important relationship between ethics and politics. Bernstein (1991) explains:

> I use the hyphenated expression "ethical-political." I do so in order to invoke and recall the classical understanding of the symbiotic relation between ethics and politics. . . . Politics is concerned with our public lives in the *polis*—with the communal bonds that at once unite and separate us as citizens. . . . Although we can distinguish ethics and politics, they are inseparable. For we cannot understand ethics without thinking through our political commitments and responsibilities. And there is no understanding of politics that does not bring us back

to ethics. Ethics and politics . . . are aspects of a unified practical philosophy. It is because ethics and politics are so intimately related that both Plato and Aristotle are so concerned with the tensions between them, and with the central question of what is the relation between leading a good life and becoming a good citizen. The scope of what the Greeks took to be the proper ethical-political domain is far broader and richer than modern understandings of morality. (p. 9)

A society's constitution, such as the Constitution of the United States, is a centrally important ethical-political document. Though the politics of a particular society, and perhaps even its laws, do not live up to its constitutional guarantees, that society is, ultimately, justified and legitimized by its basic ideals. Teachers who practice *public moral inquiry* should keep these ideals in mind, and they should have a current knowledge of their country's many legal battles to uphold and institutionalize its foundational principles.

The majority of this book's readers are, most likely, from the United States. Americans should be proud of the fact that the United States has the longest standing democratic constitution in the world today. Furthermore, the U.S. Constitution has served as a model for many other countries. The fact that many of our planet's nations justify their political existence on the basis of democratic ideals is an important referent for *public moral inquiry.*

Reciprocity

Reciprocity is an important feature of public interactions in pluralistic societies. It is based on two key principles: *everyone gets a chance to talk, and everyone must listen.* Mutual interactions are sanctioned and encouraged. No individual or group gets to dominate the public conversation in either overt or more subtle ways. There is a critical alertness to the many ways domination can manifest itself:

Domination in general may be understood as supremacy of one voice over all others. Domination . . . is defined by the singularity of one prevailing position, view, theory, doctrine, or belief. Singularity means domination, regardless of how different people perceive the prevailing voice in terms of progress,

justice, efficiency, and other normative scales. Even a just belief becomes domineering if it prevails apart from a larger dialogue. (Sidorkin, 1999, p. 34)

Public forums based on reciprocal dialogue provide a space for
the play of diverse perspectives. There is a "symphony" of distinctive, and perhaps, contradictory voices.

Just as *all* citizens must be allowed to cultivate and assert
their distinctive "voices" in the public arena, they must also be
willing to listen. Sidorkin (1999) explains: "If I want you to recognize me as a group member, there is a price attached to that:
I have to allow you to take part in defining what my group is.
The recognition of oppressed groups should involve dialogue
with the rest of society, including the oppressors" (p. 40). From
the perspective of reciprocal dialogue, the validity of an "Afro-
centric" public school, or any form of "ethnocentric" public education, must be seriously questioned. Though the justification
of an educational institution fostering a particular identity might
be made on the basis of reversing years, and perhaps even cen-
turies, of exclusionary practices, such a school may not be designed to foster reciprocal dialogue. Though reciprocal dialogue
requires sensitivity and civility (Elshtain, 1995), it cannot occur in
a climate of sanctioned defensiveness. Again, Sidorkin (1999)
writes: "The plurality of worldviews only makes sense if used for
bringing these worldviews into contact, testing them against each
other in the ever-changing context of our common lives" (p. 41).
Reciprocity is not for timid and overly protective souls; it is for
the brave and courageous citizens of a pluralistic society.

Maxine Greene's philosophic essay, *The Dialectic of Freedom* (1988) was introduced in chapter 1. An important feature
of this book is her celebration of the growth-enhancing possibilities of reciprocity. She presents a vision of a pluralistic, democratic society in which the citizens enjoy the challenges of authentic interaction:

> This is what we shall look for as we move: freedom developed
> by human beings who have acted to make a space for them-
> selves in the presence of others, human beings become "chal-
> lengers" ready for alternatives, alternatives that include caring
> and community. And we shall seek, as we go, implications for
> emancipatory education conducted by and for those willing to

take responsibility for themselves and for each other. We want
to discover how to open spaces for persons in the plurality,
spaces where they can become different, where they can
grow. (p. 56)

The type of society envisioned by Greene is one that understands the creative value of reciprocal dialogue—even among
citizens who, at best, may only be able to agree to disagree.

Social Philosophy

Public moral inquiry culminates with the construction and refinement of a social philosophy, which is defined as *a coherent
position on what constitutes the virtuous life.* A social philosophy is created when such curriculum concerns as students' moral
competencies, character development, and/or civic sensibilities
are integrated into a carefully articulated and well-defended ethical stance. Teachers who construct and continually refine their
social philosophy can explain the deep-seated "why's" of their
actions. They can justify their practices in light of what they consider to be the "higher" purposes of public education. The discussion of *teaching for democratic living* in chapter 1 serves as
a concrete illustration of a social philosophy.

Though some educators may think philosophical inquiry is
too theoretical for the practicalities of their educational craft,
Dewey (1935) argues otherwise. He points out that the construction of a social philosophy is, in fact, the most practical
thing a teacher can do:

> What will it profit a man [or woman] to do this, that, and the other
> specific thing, if he has no clear idea of why he is doing them, no
> clear idea of the way they bear upon actual conditions and of the
> end to be reached? The most specific thing that educators can first
> do is something general. The first need is to become aware of the
> kind of world in which we live; to survey its forces; to see the op-
> position in forces that are contending for mastery; to make up
> one's mind which of these forces come from a past that the world
> in its potential powers has outlived and which are indicative of a
> better and happier future. The teacher who has made up his mind
> on these points will have little difficulty in discovering for himself
> what specific things are needed in order to put into execution the
> decisions that he has arrived at. [Supreme Court] Justice Holmes

once said that theory was the most practical thing in the world. This statement is pre-eminently true of social theory of which educational theory is a part. (p. 7)

INQUIRY SCAFFOLDING

The challenge of *public moral inquiry* is to construct a guiding social philosophy that is attentive to inclusivity (social and personal justice), constitutionality (democratic ethics and politics), and reciprocity (mutual dialogue). Though this is a formidable inquiry challenge for any public educator, there are teachers who rise to the occasion. As part of their ongoing craft reflections, they are morally thoughtful and responsible (Tom, 1984). As they continuously learn through cycles of instructional study, application, observation, and reflection, they contemplate the nature of "public morality" in a diverse society with democratic ideals.

The following questions are designed as a scaffolding to support your own *public moral inquiries.* To the degree that they are helpful, they should be carefully considered. However, if they are distracting, or even inhibiting, they should be modified or even ignored. As mentioned in chapter 1, disciplined inquiry is personally idiosyncratic, and what may be useful to one person may not be useful to another. The important points to keep in mind as you examine the scaffolding are the underlying moral concerns that guided the creation of this set of questions—that is, the concerns for inclusivity, constitutionality, reciprocity, and social philosophy. Here is the scaffolding:

§ How do I distinguish between private and public morality with reference to *all* members of my society, and how does my understanding of public morality inform my sense of professional responsibility? For example, how would I define and support "family values" *without* marginalizing or condemning any social group within my society?

§ How is my teaching informed by social and personal justice concerns? In what ways are my practices "culturally responsive"?

§ Is my understanding of public morality informed by the Constitution and its legal traditions? For example, what is my position on the use of publicly funded vouchers to support private education *given* the laws of my society? What if there is conflict between these laws and customs? How should this conflict be resolved?

§ Is my understanding of public morality responsive to current social trends? In light of changing times, do I need to rethink the nature of public morality? For example, as members of my society become more environmentally aware, what are the implications for public laws? How should *we* treat other species on our planet?

§ How would I describe the democratic ethics that are practiced in my classroom?

§ How do I foster reciprocal dialogue in my classroom, in my school, and between my school and the community it serves? How would I describe the quality of my conversations with students, parents, colleagues, and other educational stakeholders? Do I allow for the play of diverse perspectives, and do I celebrate the creative possibilities of relating with different people?

§ In the spirit of John Dewey's point, discussed earlier in this chapter, that a social philosophy is "the most practical thing in the world," can I articulate and defend the ways in which my teaching practices are *principled?* For example, could I integrate my responses to all the other questions in this scaffolding into a coherent statement about the nature of the "virtuous life" that public education should support? What is my position on the best way to educate for moral competency, personal ethics, character development, and citizenship?

§ Are my teaching practices congruent with my deepest beliefs about "quality" public education, and how would I describe the ways I have integrated my public moral inquires into my daily instructional activities? In other words, how exactly do my public moral inquires guide the continuous refinement of my classroom teaching? For example, if a parent visited my class, would I be comfortable discussing the underlying values of the lesson he or she observed and how these values influenced my lesson planning?

§

Teacher Narrative*

I remember when I was a child growing up in the 1950s going with my dad to visit my mom who was recovering from a serious illness at one of the city's large hospitals. Our journey took us through the streets of the inner city. We drove by house after neglected house. I recall rolling up my car window because the acrid fowl smell of nearby factories permeated the air. Streets were strewn with debris and litter. Dilapidated porches and yards were peopled with young children and old folks. I asked Dad why conditions were so bad in this part of town. He responded that the causes were very complex but that the bottom line was that people in our city did not care enough to change things. The sight of the hospital parking lot was a welcome relief to the surrounding neighborhood. Mom's waiting embrace reassured me that she was well on the mend and that our secure, loving home would once again be complete. While driving back home through the same streets, my eyes often met the gaze of children my own age and I would think how lucky I was. My good fortune was to have been born into a place far removed from these dreadful circumstances. As Dad drove the station wagon into our neighborhood, I rolled down my window and savored the clean air and welcomed the lush green expanses that surrounded the houses. I was blessed but my mind's eye would always remember the gaze of those children.

Mom returned home and my childhood summer resumed its carefree, easy pace of countless hours scrambling up and down the beautiful wooded hillsides of the metro park that adjoined our property. There was no limit to the imaginary worlds that were created as my playmates and I trekked down the hill, through the creek, and over the bottomlands to the river. One day, as we were trying to catch "chubs" in the creek, we were overwhelmed by a disagreeable, pungent odor. We left to play elsewhere but later that day at dinner I told Mom about the smell. For several days, I watched as she monitored the back yard environs and then began calling neighbors. Something was happening to this lovely little stream, and she was going to get to the bottom of

---

*Contributed by Bridget Robbins.

it. On the fourth day, Mom picked up the phone and dialed City Hall. "What is going on?" she demanded. "I want answers!" She followed the initial call immediately with a series of phone calls to our councilman and various ward politicians. The answers came within days. A dry cleaner was illegally disposing of cleaning fluid into a storm drain that during heavy rains would flow into the creek. He was fined and shut down until proper disposal methods were installed. My friends and I returned to the creek to resume our happy pursuit of its little creatures.

As the years passed, I began to focus more of my attention and free time on the social pursuits of a typical teenager than the exploration of our natural environs. My lovely parklike backyard, however, was always there to provide a frequently needed quiet place to sort out the sometimes scrambled feelings I would encounter as heart and mind raced to keep up with body. Change was everywhere. One autumn day, as I walked home from high school, I noticed that huge bulldozers were clearing a large tract of land near the top of our street. I flashed back to the days spent with friends chasing kites, climbing trees, and fielding balls in its beautiful pastures but quickly consoled myself with thoughts of shopping convenience and progress. Our home was situated one half mile from the building site and safely ensconced in the wooded serenity of the park system—or so I thought. October's spectacular colors were followed by an early winter chill. Several weeks later, as I walked home from school calculating how many hours my brother and I would have to spend raking leaves that weekend, my eye caught an unfamiliar site on the hillside across from our backyard. "What is that?" I raced from the back door to the edge of our property to get a better view. The trees were bare and the leaves were blanketing the valley and hillside with a soft brown hue in all but one place. At the end of a steep ravine where the shopping center property abutted the park, there was a huge, ugly mass of what appeared to be debris. "Who did this?" "Why?" I ran to get Mom but found her totally preoccupied. She was on her way to the hospital. My aunt, her sister, was having emergency surgery. The next day, the mass on the hillside had grown even larger. As I walked into the house, I met Mom on her way out. The worried look in her eye told me that my aunt was still in serious condition. It was no time to ask, but still the words came out, "Mom, what can we do about this?" I pointed to the ugly grayish heaps of building debris on the far hillside. Her eyes flashed at me and she replied intensely, "Bridget, you know how to dial the phone. Take care of it!"

For years, I had observed my parents' involvement in the community. Busy lives—eight children and a family business—did not keep them from giving time, energy, and resources to improving the schools, playgrounds, churches, libraries, and, in general the physical and social environment that was our neighborhood. They attended meetings, organized and ran programs, built better recreational facilities, campaigned for good leaders, and made many phone calls to keep our neighborhood safe and attractive.

Now it was my turn. With Mom's electric charge still ringing in my ears, I picked up the phone book and phone, dialed the numbers, and, using a mature, firm voice that belied my sixteen years, queried officials at city hall. "Who gave permission to dump refuse in the ravine?" "Is the Health Department aware of this?" "How about the Department of Sanitation?" "Have the building inspectors approved this?" "If so, who was responsible?" "Why is the city allowing this?" I demanded answers. I was outraged. I was a lifelong resident of the area and was going to make sure my councilman knew who at city hall was cooperative and who was not.

The answers came. The developer was not given a permit to dump. He thought he was doing everyone a favor by filling in the ravine. He intended to cover the debris with dirt once the building phase was completed. In other words, he had found a very cheap way to dispose of trash. One week later, the debris was gone. I walked into my backyard, saw that the hillside was restored, and heard a resounding "YES!" leap from my voice. What a gift my parents had given me—years and years of civic involvement. And what a sense of empowerment Mom gave me that day when she simply said, "Take care of it!" I knew what she meant. You are not helpless. You can do this. You must get involved.

When I began my teaching career, I was determined that my students would understand that the quality of their lives in our society would in large measure be determined by their willingness to get involved and that they never need to feel helpless! They could make a difference!

The Cold War raged during my high school years. I became increasingly aware of the power of government to affect the quality of life in society. My mind reflected frequently on the contrast between my parents' experiences freely working for positive social change in our community and the stories of Eastern European émigrés from Hungary and Czechoslovakia, who lost both their struggle against communism and their voice in government. I became fascinated with the power of philosophical ideas not only to shape government and society, but also to control the extent of individual freedom and personal fulfillment. My understanding of the evolution of democratic ideals and principles, which began in high school, was expanded by the exploration of these ideas in their original form in college. In doing so, the power of social thought in creating social progress became clear to me. At this point in my life, I realized that, as a teacher, whether I taught social studies or science, transcending all course content would be a framework for stimulating the development of a social philosophy that encouraged ethical behavior and democratic ideals. I was entering the teaching profession to educate and empower young people to improve the quality of their own lives and, ultimately, the quality of life in our society as a whole.

My professional teaching career began in 1984 after a long hiatus to raise four children and build a family business. I knew that my strong academic preparation and excellent teacher training experiences would not be enough to engage this MTV generation. To complicate matters even further, I was competing with the beautiful beaches of South Carolina. I had to make connections that students could relate to in their own lives or lose them in daydreams of after-school activities. What did my students really care about that would engage them intellectually and emotionally? The answer was as clear as the salt air—the ocean, of course! With my first class of fifth graders, I used the issue of beach erosion and protection of the sand dunes as the "hot topic" that kept the students involved. They loved their beaches and wanted to know what could be done to save them. The issue allowed application in all subject areas that I was teaching—science, math, social studies, English, and art! Field trips were a pleasure to plan. We were only a block from the ocean.

The following year, I transferred to the high school and there began to embark on a very steep learning curve. My course content was strongly governed by curriculum guides born out of the Educational Improvement Agenda of Governor Riley of South Carolina. Standardized test scores were on everyone's mind. I knew that passing proficiency tests would not make my juniors better citizens, but if I could get their active attention by making connections to their own lives, they would learn more and, hopefully, care more. Rock musicians like Bob Geldorf made my job easier. Although most music of the 1980s was not political, a significant number of musicians and groups had a social conscience. Exploring the causes they were advocating opened a new energy field in classroom dialogue, discussion, and debate. Understanding the scientific, historical, and geopolitical factors that led to widespread famine, the focus of the unprecedented Band-Aid and Live-Aid concerts, became a springboard for examining the entire region in a course on world cultures. In U.S. history, studying the famine issue was a valuable tool in affirming the foundation of the American political structure, as well as in understanding the historical and contemporary development of public policy. Furthermore, the famine issue was an opportunity for students to actively engage in helping others through fund-raising activities. Music was the medium that sparked their interest. At the time, I wondered, "Would I always need to connect with pop culture?"

In addition to the active involvement of musicians in important causes, I found that students reacted positively to the efforts of student-led college organizations in the dismantling of apartheid. The lobbying efforts of young people to influence their universities to divest, businesses to withdraw, and our government to impose sanctions became a compelling starting point for examining and debating the historical and contemporary development of U.S. civil rights. Segregation in our recent past took on added significance after examining the experiences of Nelson Mandela, Stephen Biko, and Desmund Tutu. Students followed the issue in the press and posted articles detailing accounts of raids and detentions on our classroom bulletin board. I was surprised by the depth of their interest. They were especially concerned about the number of young children who were incarcerated in an attempt to silence dissent. Many of my students joined in letter-writing campaigns to lobby businesses and the federal government to pressure South Africa to reform. In all of this, they were learning so much about their own precious rights and freedoms. They were developing a deeper sensitivity to the entire issue of intolerance. The Confederate flag flying over the state capitol became a lightning rod for discussion and debate.

During my first year at the high school, the administration asked that I develop and coach a Mock Trial team to compete in a nationwide competition run by the American Bar Association. Although I had studied constitutional law, I had no experience in courtroom procedure and was not looking forward to the additional responsibilities. My priority was the classroom. I had no idea how much this experience was about to impact my classroom teaching. Lacking legal training, I wasted no time in lining up attorneys to advise us. Student interest was strong. They loved the idea of taking a case—civil or criminal—tearing it apart, analyzing it, studying the legal precedents, and then preparing both sides of the case for trial. Countless hours were spent in studying, researching, documenting, writing briefs, exploring affidavits, developing direct and cross exams, writing opening statements, and developing closing arguments. Practices were long and demanding. I marveled at how hard these students worked, how motivated they were, and how much they learned. Why? What made them commit such energy to learning outside the classroom? How could this continuous flow of dedication be transferred to within the classroom? The challenge of the competition was very important. However, it was more than this that kept them coming to endless meetings and practices. They were fascinated with the many experts from the community that came to our meetings to share their knowledge—detectives, weapons specialists, psychologists, criminologists, prosecutors, public defenders, to name a few. I prevailed on the expertise of my colleagues in English, drama, math, and science. Whatever it took to understand and prepare the case for trial. Students loved the fresh perspective brought by the advising teachers. In the end, however, the students made the decisions about how the case was developed. I believed it to be critical that the team members, after analyzing all the possible options, made the decision on what theories of the case to pursue. From the very beginning, the students understood that, win or lose, it was their case. They were invested. They had ownership.

In 1986, our first, very dedicated team lost in the first round at the district level. Not to be discouraged, those who had not graduated came back the following year, shared their expertise with new team members, and won the state semifinals. In 1988, the team not only won the state competition but prepared an entirely new case in less than three weeks and won the American Bar Association's National Mock Trial competition held that year in Dallas, Texas.

The excellence in learning that this program engendered was something I wanted in my classroom. The self-motivation and excitement that elicited high-level, analytical and critical thinking skills, oral advocacy, and written briefs was an educator's dream. I was trying to figure out how to incorporate this type of role-playing into my teaching when a good friend and colleague asked me to help her take a few students to Princeton University's Model Congress in Washington, DC. I had learned so much about effective teaching from the

Mock Trial program—the excitement of the role-play, an issue to research and debate, the satisfaction and enthusiasm that stemmed from student-led case analysis and development—that I decided to give it a try. Again, I was amazed. Prior to the conference, students identified national issues about which they were concerned, researched and analyzed extensively, wrote legislation to address the public policy issue, studied Robert's Rules of Order, and formally debated the merits of their bill in model congress sessions.

Some of their areas of concern were far beyond my level of expertise. I had to rely once again on the help of colleagues and experts from the community. Students were developing policy on programs for defense, foreign aid, trade, science and technology research, the environment, education, welfare reform, and tax relief, to name a few. They spent hours researching, wrote letters to their congressman, and requested briefing papers from the congressional committee responsible for studying an issue. I required that each bill be examined and approved first by a teacher or professional knowledgeable in the field, then by an English teacher for grammatical correctness, and, finally, by me, for constitutionality.

The effort students put forth in preparation was only a prelude to the rigorous pace of the Model Congress itself. Following the teacher approval process, each bill was sent off to the Princeton Whig Society, where it was bound into a bill book for the Model Congress. Students arrived in Washington, DC, from across the United States. At registration, they each received a bill book containing copies of all the submitted legislation. I watched in awe as 600 young people, having developed considerable expertise, intelligently debated public policy for four days from 8:30 A.M. to 9:30 P.M. in a model congress format. It was exhilarating to be in a forum with so much creativity being expended to design programs that would improve the quality of life in our nation. Students had ample opportunity to present their bills, deliver formal speeches, and defend the need to change the status quo in small committee sessions chaired by members of the Princeton Whig Society. They quickly learned the need to build consensus and coalitions. Those bills that made it out of committee went to full congressional sessions presided over by senior student staff members. Any bill approved by both houses of the model congress was sent to the actual Congress and White House. What my students experienced was four days of total immersion in national policy issues and legislative development. They were not exhausted. They were excited. On the way home, they made plans for what they wanted to work on for next year's congress.

The eight-hour trip home was a great opportunity to reflect on the events of the past four days. I had learned so much about substantive issues—B2 bombers, foreign aid to China, deficit spending, debt reduction, educational reform, Arab–Israeli relations, capital gains taxes, flat taxes, health care reform, welfare reform, environmental protection, NASA missions, sterling engines, fuel efficiency and energy research, AIDS research, genetic engineering—just to name a few. More important, my students learned. It was an information explosion, not just about issues, but about the whole democratic process. What really struck me was that the entire experience was student centered. This was a role-play that not only interned young people in the theory and practice of democracy, but challenged them to use their own creativity to design the solutions to our nation's problems. They had a sense of ownership about their own education. They were beginning to see themselves as lifelong learners, which was one of the most important goals in my classroom. My colleague and I discussed various strategies for implementing the format. By the end of the trip, we knew what we were going to do. We would design several new issues-centered courses. One, a national issues course, would be built on the model congress format. The second, an international issues course, would use a model United Nations format. Fortunately, my colleague was also the department chair. We received speedy approval and registered our first classes in the spring.

When the first class convened, I made sure that my students understood their responsibilities to the process. It was their work that we would be debating, and it would require quality research and documentation. More important, they would be running the class. (In Washington, I realized that the students were energized not only by debating their own public policy proposals, but by the democratic process, as well.) The class would be an exercise in democracy. Each session would be run by a student chairperson according to Robert's Rules. We spent the first three weeks of the semester researching and documenting issues in the media center. Students had chosen topics that involved almost every discipline. Teachers from other departments were most helpful in supplying useful information and guidance. They were excited about the fact that these students were understanding the relationship of their studies to the public policy that affects all of our lives. My mailbox was always full.

We began to network resources. Students wrote members of Congress, contacted experts in the executive departments, and followed every credible lead in the information discovery process. The need for each piece of legislation had to be validated by the student in a documented 4–5-page (minimum) fact sheet. Once the legislation was written in proper bill format, it was published in a bill book. Students had to prepare formal speeches supporting and opposing legislation. Four weeks into the semester, we were ready to begin. They loved it! They came to class excited and prepared. They were continuously researching the credibility of the public policy under consideration. Each day, I marveled at the quality of debate and the sincerity of the young people involved.

In all of the years that I taught the class, there were only two occasions in which I found it necessary to intervene. Regarding the first, students were debating a bill that would tie federal funds for crime prevention to strict mandatory sentencing guidelines set by the state. It became apparent that several of my students were emotionally distressed. Beneath the thin veneer of their formal speeches, I could surmise that there was personal involvement because of abuse in the family. Using Robert's Rules and without calling attention to the people involved, I made a motion to "postpone debate" until experts from CASA (Citizens Against Spousal Abuse) and the county prosecutor's office could come in to offer testimony. The community officials responded quickly, came to class, and shared their expertise on "battered-spouse syndrome," which then helped the class amend the bill to develop a more effective and humane public policy. After class, two of the students shared their personal family stories with me, and I directed them to school guidance and CASA counselors.

During the second semester of 1988, the vast majority of students in the class chose to research and write policy on environmental issues. There was a reason for this. Ocean pollution had driven the environmental crisis to the forefront in our community. My students and their families were experiencing the effects of contaminated syringes and vials washing up on shore, high bacteria counts from nonpoint source pollution, oil slicks and recreational boating debris, destruction of saltwater marshes, and declining fish populations. The issues selected for research included air and water pollution, toxic-waste disposal, solid-waste disposal, biodiversity, rain forest destruction, wetlands destruction, endangered species, ocean dumping, destruction of the ozone layer, and clear cutting in the national forests. Committee hearings and debate explored the magnitude of the these problems and the complexity of finding solutions. During debate on the bill addressing ocean pollution, I again motioned to "postpone debate." At this point, I asked that the author of the legislation invite to class experts from the Coastal Council to explain local programs being developed to address the issue. I recommended that the authors of each of the remaining bills do the same, that is, find local experts to come to class and explain the current status of efforts to solve the problem. This proved very informative, but in every case added to the documentation that students had already compiled on the enormity of the crisis. The class continued with debate and passed legislation that would improve the nation's commitment to preserving the environment; however, my students took no satisfaction in this role-play. They knew the issues as well as the experts and they knew the solutions, but they had no power to do anything to stop the clock ticking on environmental devastation. They were overwhelmed by public apathy and their own helplessness.

My greatest concern was that the malaise the students were developing would cause them to "disconnect"—to turn away from the system. Role-playing was not enough. Believing they could do too little too late, they would simply disassociate from the problems and the process. I talked with the class about their concerns. I reflected that adults with similar concerns would join environmental organizations or advocacy groups. Several days later, I asked the class how they would feel about forming an environmental organization at school to address some of these issues. The lights went on! Immediately, we began to brainstorm how the group would be run. The class was eager to advertise and recruit members. From the onset, I insisted that the weekly meetings be action oriented. No endless discussions on what we were going to do. We would be taking concrete steps every week to improve the environment!

In September of 1988, the beginning of the new school year, the organization met for the first time. We had decided to meet after school in the media center to have access to databases for research. When I walked into the library for the first meeting, I was overwhelmed! Every chair was taken. Students were sitting on the floor, on bookcases, anywhere there was space. Over 125 high school students had turned out, eager to get started. It was exhilarating to see so many young people concerned and ready to work. After a few introductory remarks by myself and former members of the class, we broke into committees and brainstormed the areas on which we would focus our efforts. The meeting concluded with a large group session in which the entire organization chose the agenda for the year. Permanent committees were formed and students decided on which committees they would serve.

Each week when I walked to the library for our meeting, I expected the crowd to abate. It did not. From the very beginning, I could not keep up with the number of ideas and programs developed by these young people. They researched, documented, presented their ideas, and then took action. We were joined by teachers from every department. Experts from the community frequently joined us to lend their expertise. Community organizations, such as the League of Women Voters, Sierra Club, National Wildlife Federation, and Coastal Council, kept us informed on local projects and important national issues. We began to network extensively. The Legislative Committee had begun lobbying campaigns to urge recycling efforts by federal and state governments, prohibit clear cutting in the national forests, prevent the relocation of a radioactive waste site to a nearby county with a high water table, and reduce dioxin contamination in a nearby river. The Education Committee was committed to spreading the word. Their efforts were focused primarily on young school children. They wrote, directed, and performed an environmental play and puppet show to the delight of elementary and middle school students. Each year, they were asked to perform for our community's Earth Day celebration. They designed and ran a poster contest for children in our system's twenty-six elementary schools to culminate the teaching of an environmental unit that they had prepared and distributed to teachers. To help facilitate the protection of our precious sea turtle population, they designed and distributed educational brochures for tourists, to help them identify and protect new nests. Water quality testing and monitoring was done by our Pollution Committee, many of whom were surfers and very troubled by high bacteria counts and oil slicks.

They recruited large numbers of members to participate in annual community programs such as Beach Sweep, Springtide, and Swampfest. The Recycling Committee introduced in-house recycling programs and then began researching the feasibility of a districtwide (38 schools, 40,000 students) recycling program for office paper. Their efforts required them to make presentations to the school board and county council. After six months of negotiating with the world's third largest paper recycler, the county council, and the school district, thirty-eight schools began to recover their used office and school paper. At the end of the process, two of the students were asked to join the county's new solid-waste management advisory board.

In November of 1990, the League of Women Voters presented an informational forum on dioxin contamination to our organization. Scientists from a coastal research facility described studies that had been conducted on nearby estuaries and rivers. One river was so heavily contaminated with dioxin that detailed warnings had been posted by the Department of Health and Environmental Control (DHEC), stating that the fish were contaminated and should not be eaten. My students were especially concerned when they learned that most of the people fishing the river were subsistence fishermen, many of whom were illiterate and whose catches represented a major portion of their family's diet. Following the League's presentation, our organization began its own investigation. An intense study was undertaken by four students. After interviewing executives from the paper mill, commercial fishermen, subsistence fishermen, physicians, pharmacists, local residents, and the head of the Environmental Protection Agency's (EPA) toxic division in Washington, DC, by phone, the students published their findings in a seventy-five-page report, which they presented to our organization in January of 1991. As the employer of 900 people, the company that was responsible for the pollution was a key player in the economic life of the community. It had been granted permits to exceed federal EPA emissions guidelines for over ten years. Pollution prevention equipment was expensive. However, profits for this international corporation were almost $400 million that year. Still, the mill was applying for another permit to exceed standards. State public hearings on the permit were to be held in late February of 1991.

It was a very busy month. Students were running a number of programs. I realized, driving to the hearing site, which was one hour away, that I had not inquired who would be attending. To my surprise, twenty-five of my students were already seated in the auditorium when I arrived. Fifteen of these students had signed the speakers list. Members of the DHEC review board were seated on stage. The microphone for public comment was positioned below the stage. Directly in front of the microphone were four full rows of businessmen and officers from the company all dressed in dark suits. Opening comments were followed by a number of speeches given by company employees and scientists from high-profile universities. A few timid residents and fishermen spoke. And then the students started. Each one was articulate and logical. There were no accusations, no indictments. They simply shared what they had learned and asked for reason to prevail. They were eloquent.

The permit to exceed standards was denied. The company was given a timetable to install the pollution control equipment. In 1992, the South Carolina Wildlife Federation awarded our organization its Youth Conservationist Award for its efforts in the elimination of dioxin contamination and the establishment of community recycling programs. The awards dinner was exciting, and the students were elated. However, no award ceremony would ever eclipse the overwhelming sense of pride and respect for these young people that I was privileged to experience on the night of the hearing. I realized how much they had changed my life. In working through this problem together, we had moved from social awareness to social action and effective citizenship. I would be forever grateful to these young people and forever searching for ways to more successfully integrate opportunities for student-initiated social action into the existing curriculum.

In 1992, my dad became seriously ill, and I began to explore the possibility of moving closer to him in order to help with his care. It was extremely difficult to leave South Carolina. My decision was made easier by the fact that my children were already living in the Midwest for college and professional careers. Finding a job in a school district with a reputation for high standards and quality performance, however, was key to making the move. In 1993, I accepted a position in an outstanding district in Ohio. It was in a picture-perfect little town that served as a "bedroom" community for middle- and upper-class business and professional people working in nearby cities. It was very different from the heterogeneous, eclectic beach environment that I had been teaching in. I was excited about getting started. New job, new environs, new challenges!

After two weeks of exhausting work, I felt like I had hit "a wall," or more accurately "a bubble." Most of my students were totally disassociated from the problems of the world, country, even their own region. Their parents had provided a perfectly ideal environment, and they could not relate to a social philosophy or the need for social action. They were in a "bubble." Society's problems, as far as they were concerned, did not affect them. Their hamlet was secure.

They were, however, motivated to do well in school. Their parents had instilled in them the economic value of a good education, and they were extremely grade conscious. I was now teaching young people who would study and learn, but had little vision of civic consciousness. They were not impacted by environmental degradation. Such problems were remote. Furthermore, they could not comprehend the debilitating effects of poverty. If a person in our society was not doing well, they felt it was solely the result of not working hard! The challenge for me in my teaching the district-mandated curriculum for U.S. history and government was to enable my students to see the relationship between society's problems and the quality of their own lives in our democracy. They had to understand the effects in order to care. I had to get them out of the "bubble."

I began the process by introducing issues research and debate. This had been successful in the past not only in developing an awareness of, but in stimulating interest in contemporary social problems. The district-mandated curriculum began with the study of U.S. history in the late-nineteenth century. First, I had students research the progressive era, then compare and contrast the problems of the 1890s with those of the 1990s. Next, they were to analyze progressive reforms and the impact they have had on the quality of life today. Finally, they had to choose one contemporary problem, research it extensively, and then propose a reform measure. Each proposal would be examined in a model senate committee hearing with a student chair. In choosing the issue to be researched, the student was taking ownership. It was his or her problem to solve. The role-play was successful. The class was clearly engaged in understanding the research that was presented, and the policy ideas that were suggested. More important, the students began to see the connection between the issues—poverty, crime, drugs, violence, racism, health care, urban sprawl, environmental degradation—and their own lives.

The process began to stimulate some creative ideas and exchanges. I had also introduced the model senate concept for issues research and debate in my U.S. government class. One of my seniors, who was researching health care reform, discussed the issue with one of my U.S. history students. In doing so, they thought it would be useful to have professionals in the health care industry explain their views on the proposals actually under consideration. I concurred and suggested that they plan a forum in which the health care professionals would present to all the classes. Of course, their time and efforts would offset other homework/research requirements. After weeks of planning, the students brought together representatives from HMOs, pharmaceutical firms, and hospitals, doctors, nurses, and our own congressional representative for a forum on health care reform. The entire process was handled by the students, including the introductions and question/answer sessions.

My students were beginning to make the connection between certain issues and their own lives. They could understand the impact of 40 million uninsured on their own health care costs; they understood the cost of crime, substance abuse, and a failed welfare system in tax dollars paid out by their families. However, I wanted them to care about others less fortunate. I believed that, unless they cared, it would be easy to dismiss or get caught up in the routine of their busy lives and not work to effect positive change, except to vote for those who promised less government and lower taxes. Readings from Jonathan Kozol's *Savage Inequalities* and *Amazing Grace* provided an excellent springboard for discussions of the vicious cycle of poverty, drugs, and crime. Exploring the lives of young children growing up in East St. Louis or the South Bronx was a reality check for what my students had been given as a birthright. Ron Kotulka, a science writer for the *Chicago Tribune*, had done a series of articles covering the most recent research on how the brain develops and the effects that violence has on this development. As a class, we studied the information, then brainstormed the implications for kids growing up in East St. Louis, the South Bronx, or other similar environs. They began to understand that poverty and violence rob the soul not just the body—that we are not all born on a level playing field.

In 1995, I was teaching economics, as well as U.S. history and government. My students could understand the interdependence of the global economy but knew little of the connection between regional economic and social problems. And although many of my students in history and government were beginning to connect to social justice issues, the relationship was distant. I discussed this with a colleague, and we began to brainstorm ways in which the study of these issues could connect them more closely to the historical, economic, social, environmental, and cultural development of their own region. We wanted them to understand that the problems of the nearby inner cities were our problems, as well—that, although insulated, our community was not isolated. Even our school district was feeling the impact of urban "outmigration" and an overburdened tax base. What we created was a program of "alternative assessment," known as Urban Studies, that would allow students to choose one of a series of projects and demonstrations to develop and present in place of their ninety-minute semester exam. The projects would offer a variety of media for presentation and readily engage all learning styles. Our principal was very supportive of the idea and we prevailed on the good graces and expertise of a recently retired "master" teacher to help us with the program. In all, twenty-seven projects, including one that allowed the student the option of designing his/her own project, were offered that would connect the students through various issues with our geographic region. My favorite project idea was project 27, which required students to volunteer twenty-four hours over the course of the semester in an inner-city agency, such as a homeless shelter, soup kitchen, food bank, community center, or Head Start. In addition to the twenty-four hours on site, students were required to write a reaction paper that reflected on their experience.

My colleague and I introduced the program to our classes at the onset of the 1995 school year. The response was overwhelming. Over 25 percent of the students in my classes chose to do alternative assessment. Much to my surprise and delight, the vast majority had chosen project 27. I believed that this project more than any other would make a lasting impression on them. It was my guess that they believed it was a great way out of my lengthy semester exam. I indulged them in this. I was getting twenty-four hours on site (travel time not included), three journal readings, and a reaction paper. For me, it was a "no brainer." My unit tests were sufficiently challenging. They did not lack for test-taking experience. I was getting a total of 35–40 hours of commitment in place of 5–6 hours of review study time.

My only concern was the time involved in reading and evaluating the reaction papers at the end of the term. Little did I know what was in store for me. As soon as the students started into the agency experience, they began to share stories with the class. After four or five visits, there was an excitement projected that was contagious. Other students would accompany their classmates to see what this was all about. Most of the students were working at Head Start facilities, soup kitchens, and community centers, where children and families were involved. The discussions relating to issues took on a new dimension in class. I was aware that this was truly making a difference in my students lives, but I did not know how great the impact was until I read their reaction papers. When I sat down to the stack of papers at the end of the term, I was prepared for a long, arduous task. What I found instead was the sheer joy one experiences in reading the sincere, deliberate reflection of students who are detailing how their lives have been forever changed. Most papers began with accounts of first experiences at the agency, the length of the trip, their feelings of fear and insecurity in this new situation, and their first real personal connection with the people they were serving. They wrote about how, in the beginning, they believed they were doing so much for others but quickly moved to the amazing impact these people, especially the little ones, had on their lives. It was apparent that the change was profound. Students would write about how much they respected the children they worked with, and how cheerful and happy they were despite the fact they had little by way of material possessions—how they cared for and loved one another. They described how, instead of dreading the lengthy drive, they eagerly looked forward to their visits. Some of the observations of homeless families were especially poignant. One student reflected on a family of five—a father and four daughters, one of whom was the student's age—that came to her soup kitchen routinely one winter. Her feelings of sympathy for this teenager's embarrassment soon evaporated into respect and admiration for the love that was demonstrated within this family week after week. My student confided how she craved these close relationships in her own life.

Many of the students working in homeless shelters observed young mothers with small children, and realized how fortunate they were simply by birthright. Students frequently heard from homeless men to value education and, more important, to stay away from drugs. What the papers reflected was that these students had experienced first hand the issues we were discussing, and in that experience, their lives had been transformed. They observed unmistakably the connection between poverty and education. They recognized that the wealthiest society on earth could not survive long as a healthy democracy if it turned away from a large percentage of its most precious resources: its people, especially its beautiful children. Most important, they realized that by giving of themselves personally, how much more they had received.

The following year, many of my new students chose the Urban Studies program, in particular, project 27; and a large number of my former students continued to volunteer. Agency supervisors wrote of the positive impact these young people were having on the people they were serving as well as on the agency itself. I was beginning to feel that the "bubble" was disappearing. Many of my students were not only developing a greater understanding of social issues, they were developing greater self-awareness and self-confidence. It was satisfying to see this personal transformation taking place at the same time they were beginning to understand the effects of public policy on the social environment. They now realized, for example, how budget cuts in Head Start programs would affect the present and future lives of the little ones they were working with. There was a sense of "humanity" building, and it felt very good. The individual experiences in volunteering had produced a consciousness of social issues. My hope was that the volunteering would help to develop the citizenship necessary to effect positive social action or policy development.

In 1996, my principal asked me to attend a state "Learn and Serve" meeting with three other members of our school community. I could not refuse him. He was one of those rare breeds who was both supportive and creative. If I was working hard, he was working even harder. After the usual introductory presentations and break-out sessions, participants at this meeting were to choose from a variety of options for site visits to observe how various districts were implementing the latest educational craze—service learning. I was already "maxed out" and not looking for anything new to do. Quite frankly, I was pretty amazed that what I already was doing with Urban Studies was considered a form of service learning.

I chose to visit a nationally recognized program in a suburban district approximately forty miles from our town. We met in the city hall rather than the school, and the presentation was conducted entirely by students and the agency representatives serviced by them. I was "bowled over," to say the least. The student presentations were outstanding. They described the high-caliber, interdisciplinary program that formed the basis of their service learning course. Three days a week in a three-period classroom block, these seniors studied English and social studies. Two days a week, they were engaged in service at a community agency to which they had been assigned at the beginning of the semester. What impressed me so very much was that the relationship of what was being studied in the classroom to what was being experienced at the agency was genuine and effective. The students stressed that the universal themes in classical and contemporary literature and the philosophical basis of American government that they studied were affirmed and deepened by the agency experience. Structured by the academic program, the agency experience was the most powerful learning process they had ever had. The various agency representatives who spoke could not say enough about these young people, the program, and, what it meant, not only to their agency, but to the entire community. I had a lot to think about on the trip home.

For forty miles, my mind raced. Fortunately, my driving was more controlled. What I had just seen was the end result of tremendous efforts on the part of two very dedicated teachers. I knew the countless hours of planning, coordination, and careful administration that it took to produce. I had to tell my principal about this program, and I knew exactly what he would say, "When do we get started?" How would I respond? I could certainly tell him that I was already overextended and that he would have to find someone else. Is that what I wanted? Did I want to miss this exceptional opportunity? Isn't this exactly what I had been envisioning for my classroom over the years: civic responsibility, students learning about social issues, and students actively working through our democratic institutions to improve our society. In the past when I got involved with Mock Trial and Model Congress, didn't those programs enhance, indeed simplify, my classroom teaching? Didn't the student commitment involved in those formats energize the classroom and make my teaching far less burdensome, much more creative and rewarding? Wasn't this a program that would give my students first-hand experience in the community—indeed help them to build lifetime connections to the community? Did I want satisfaction? What would be the most satisfying course of action for me? I could not take any time from my family. That was absolute. What would I give up or trade off for this new program?

In 1998, after one year of careful planning and grant writing, and due in large measure to the able efforts of a dedicated administrator and colleague, we introduced our first Service Learning program to a class of twenty-five seniors. My colleague and I organized the curriculum (government, contemporary issues, and British literature) around four unifying themes. The themes were:

- The Evolution of Democratic Values and Ideals (first quarter)
- The Role of the Citizen in Society (second quarter)
- The Role of Social Institutions in Society (third quarter)
- Societal versus Individual Rights (fourth quarter)

We allowed for the interdisciplinary teaching of our subjects, as well as the integration of the service experiences. I was very concerned about integrating the required British literature with American government and contemporary issues and believed that this would be a Herculean task. It was not. On the contrary, it was a pleasure. There was a wealth of classical and contemporary works from which to choose. In the end, my only problem was that there was too much material, and we had to be selective.

As in the model I had observed in 1997, our students spent three days a week in a three-hour classroom block and two days a week providing services in a community agency. Students were required not only to keep a journal on their agency experience, but also to design and implement a project for their agency that would provide lasting benefits. We had students placed in twenty-four different agencies, each with an agency supervisor who evaluated their performance. Their projects invested them directly in the organization. I was not prepared for the quality and scope of the projects these young people developed. For Head Start facilities, community centers, and schools, students developed and taught units of study, arranged guest speakers and field trips, engaged children in writing, performed in other children's plays and puppet shows, and developed interagency programs in which the children performed for the elderly in nursing homes. At the science museum and metro parks, they developed hands-on exhibits for young people and educational/promotional videos. One of our students who, while working at a home for severely physically and mentally handicapped children, observed how much they enjoyed music, wrote a grant for a "bell choir" so that these children might participate more fully in the pleasure of making music. The agency was awarded the grant. The same student, while at her second-semester site, developed and coordinated an outreach program for five inner-city elementary schools that engaged the services of a social worker and child psychologist in a presentation and discussion on child abuse. This young lady gave new meaning to the "genius within" each of us. She had struggled with learning disabilities for years and in the end was teaching her teachers.

The agencies benefited enormously from the fresh perspective, high energy, and new ideas of these young people. The students were engaged in a process that would transform their lives. They learned from their supervisors; they learned from their teachers; they learned from each other; but most important, they learned from the people they served. They brought those lessons back to the classroom where they enriched our curriculum.

The ideas we discussed became real. Their own personal growth was measured in tremendous leaps of self-confidence and self-awareness. They could sense that this was happening. They also knew that something very special was building within our class because, as we were making connections to the greater community of our region, our class was building a special community of its own, one that we were all privileged to experience. We were not just talking about democracy; we were living it! We were not just talking about public morality; we were practicing it!

REFERENCES

Bernstein, R. J. (1991). *The new constellation: The ethical-political horizons of modernity/postmodernity.* Cambridge, MA: MIT Press.

Delpit, L. (1995). *Other people's children.* New York: New Press.

Dewey, J. (1935). The teacher and his world. *The Social Frontier, 1* (4), 7.

Eisner, E. W. (1994). *Cognition and curriculum reconsidered* (2nd ed.). New York: Teachers College Press.

Elshtain, J. B. (1995). *Democracy on trial.* New York: BasicBooks.

Greene, M. (1988). *The dialectic of freedom.* New York: Teachers College Press.

Kanpol, B. (1994). *Critical pedagogy: An introduction.* Westport, CT: Bergin & Garvey.

Kozol, J. (1991). *Savage inequalities: Children in America's schools.* New York: Crown.

Kozol, J. (1995). *Amazing grace: The lives of children and the conscience of a nation.* New York: Crown.

Ladson-Billings, G. (1995). But that's just good teaching! The case for culturally relevant teaching. *Theory into Practice, 34,* 159–165.

Sidorkin, A. M. (1999). *Beyond discourse: Education, the self, and dialogue.* Albany, NY: State University of New York Press.

Tom, A. (1984). *Teaching as a moral craft.* New York: Longman.

CHAPTER 3

MULTIPERSPECTIVE INQUIRY

❦

Sally McMaster sat at the dinner table lost in thought, oblivious to the television program that was blaring in the next room. Shortly after being hired as an English teacher at Fairlawn High School, her principal asked her to serve as the coach for the school's debate team. She enthusiastically assumed this responsibility. Fairlawn students had won the statewide debate contest on three occasions—a triumph that was duly noted on all road signs welcoming drivers into the city of Fairlawn. Though she felt nervous about the high level of expectations for the team, she was quite proud of the fact that she had been asked to coach the team.

Sally had started her coaching responsibilities about three weeks ago, and the students were already looking forward to the state contest that would begin in about four months. Though most of the students on the team already possessed polished debating skills, Sally felt a little uneasy. She thought to herself, "Yes, the students know the mechanics of a good debate; and yes, such knowledge was sufficient for the state contest; but did they really understand the value of the debating process? Were they too preoccupied with winning? Was their thinking too black and white? Are they learning to take positions on complex issues without an honest consideration of alternative perspectives?"

Such thoughts preoccupied Sally for an important personal reason. Her dad had been a local politician for part of his life. He would take certain political positions that, privately, he would acknowledge were too simplistic. His only defense was that politics required him to give formulaic answers to complex questions. He would say that he couldn't afford to be a statesman—that if he did so, he wouldn't politically survive. He felt he had to be simple-minded when functioning in the public arena; otherwise, his constituency would either not understand him or would find him disloyal. His only choice was to uphold the party line.

While growing up and, particularly, while preparing to become a teacher, Sally felt uncomfortable about this cynical part of her father's political realism. She felt that, oftentimes, life didn't have easy or simple answers and that teachers should prepare their students to understand and work with the complexities they encountered. She made sure that students honestly considered diverse perspectives in her English classes. Could she expect anything less from the members of the debate team? There must be something she could do to help them understand the many subtleties of complex issues and to appreciate the value of diverse points of view. But what? If the goal of a debate was to take one side of an argument and win, the only purpose for considering alternative perspectives was to point out weaknesses and inconsistencies. The goal was to function like a good lawyer and tear down your opponent's argument!

While absorbed in these questions at the dinner table, Sally's thoughts wandered to some of her professional colleagues. Listening to these teachers discuss educational issues, she often felt that their thinking was too simplistic—too black and white. They were quick to categorize and stereotype many of their students. They often responded to complex educational questions with clichés and slogans. Sally felt uncomfortable with their narrow and shallow opinions, and she would look for appropriate times to challenge their views by diplomatically offering alternative perspectives. She found that she treated these teachers much like she treated her students in her English classes—by being provocative in a patient manner.

Suddenly, Sally was struck by an intuitive insight! What if, as part of the debate team's practices, she was to create a different type of "contest." What if she would select a complex issue to discuss, and the "winner" of this discussion would be the student who could most playfully and imaginatively address all sides of the topic? She excitedly started thinking about a good issue for this contest. She also gave some thought to what it meant to "win" such a contest and what would be an appropriate prize for the "winner." She realized that she would have to carefully explain to her students her reasons for conducting at least some of their debate practices in this way. She would also, of course, need to share her rationale with the principal.

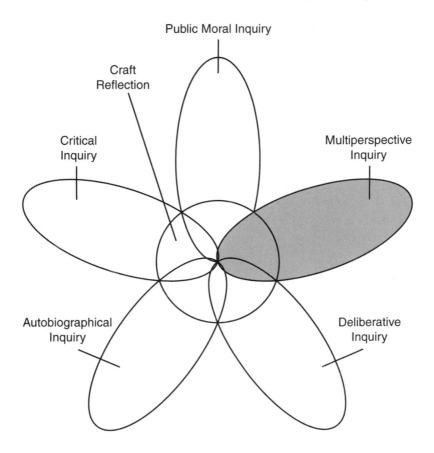

Public Moral Inquiry

Craft
Reflection

Critical
Inquiry

Multiperspective
Inquiry

Autobiographical
Inquiry

Deliberative
Inquiry

Hopefully, everyone would see the value of her instructional approach. The students would still be sharpening their debate skills, but they would be doing it in a way that would be more educationally beneficial. They would be learning how to win structured debate contests, but they would also be preparing themselves to address life's complexities in sophisticated, responsible, and creative ways.

INTRODUCTION

In this chapter, our attention turns to *multiperspective inquiry*. This is an open-ended form of disciplined professional study that explores the *uniqueness* and *complexity* of human perceptions in a *playful* frame of mind. Through multiperspective inquiry, teachers become more attentive to the multiple dimensions of their work and to the thoughts and feelings of others. As they explore diverse viewpoints, they challenge their egocentric tendencies and broaden their horizons. They learn that the world does not revolve around their perceptions and that ideological diversity is a central feature of educational work.

THREE CHARACTERISTICS OF MULTIPERSPECTIVE INQUIRY

We begin this chapter by examining three important characteristics of multiperspective inquiry: (1) sensitivity to unique perceptions, (2) tolerance for complexity, and (3) openness to intellectual play.

Uniqueness

Multiperspective inquiry begins with the recognition that there are, indeed, unique perspectives to be studied. Because human beings do not think and feel in the same ways, distinctive style and voice is an important feature of the teaching-learning process. When individual expression is discouraged, inhibited, or suppressed in the classroom, much of the color and passion of education is lost. Maxine Greene (1986) calls upon educators to honor and cultivate personal identity:

> I would like to think of teachers moving the young into their own interpretations of their lives and their lived worlds, opening wider and wider perspectives as they do so. . . . I would like to see teachers tapping the spectrum of intelligences, encouraging multiple readings of written texts and readings of the world. . . . Such a project demands the capacity to unveil and disclose. It demands the exercise of imagination, enlivened by works of art, by situations of speaking and making. . . . Perhaps we can invent ways of freeing people to feel and express indignation, to break through the opaqueness, to refuse the silences. We need to teach in such a way as to arouse passion now and then. . . . (p. 441)

Working with democratic ideals in education requires this sensitivity to personal perspective and passion. Sidorkin (1999) writes that "democracy implies lengthy discussions, ability to listen, compromise, see things through the eyes of the other" (p. 66). Simply stated, when conformity is fostered, democracy is inhibited. If teachers do not develop their capacity to "confirm" the unique voices of their students in caring ways (Noddings, 1984), they are simply not in a position to teach for democratic living.

Complexity

Multiperspective inquiry also sensitizes educators to the complexities of their work. *Teaching for democratic living* is not a simple-minded undertaking. Teachers who are committed to this way of working with their students must be comfortable with ambiguity and uncertainty. They cannot function as true believers and narrow ideologues. They must continuously stretch their minds, refine their beliefs, and acknowledge the multifaceted nature of their instructional practices. They must recognize that everything in life is not black and white and that much of education is cloaked in shades of gray. Sidorkin (1999) captures the spirit of multiperspective inquiry when he writes: "Every truth has its variations of human meanings, every truth was once disputed, and will be disputed again" (p. 125).

As mentioned in chapter 1, Pinar, Reynolds, Slattery, and Taubman (1995) argue that democratically oriented educators must approach their curriculum and teaching work as an "extraordinarily complicated conversation" incorporating many considerations (p. 848). They explain:

> We . . . regard the school curriculum as a provocation to reflect on and to think critically about ourselves, our families, our society. The point of the school curriculum is not to succeed in making us specialists in the academic disciplines. The point of the school curriculum is to goad us into caring for ourselves and our fellow human beings, to help us think and act with intelligence, sensitivity, and courage . . . as citizens aspiring to establish a democratic society and . . . as individuals committed to other individuals. (p. 848)

Teachers cannot view their work in this expansive way *unless* they are willing to practice multiperspective inquiry.

Intellectual Play

The acknowledgment of the *uniqueness* and *complexity* of human perceptions is facilitated through a *playful* consideration of diverse perspectives. When we openly compare and contrast differing points of view, we confront our basic beliefs. We challenge ourselves to broaden our horizons and to adopt more fluid positions. By playing with multiple standpoints, we refine our awareness and cultivate a more multilayered sense of life. We shed our simple selves for more sophisticated identities. Gallagher (1992) explains:

> The possibility of losing oneself or transcending oneself in play is attractive or alluring only because of the possibility of finding oneself again. I can let myself be taken up by the game, I can immerse myself in the spirit of play, only because I know that at some point I will reemerge transformed. The self lost in play does not disappear altogether. Play is productive for the self rather than destructive. Insofar as play is educational experience, the player risks herself to acquire an openness for new experiences. The result is transformation. (p. 50)

Sidorkin (1999) describes the willingness to play with perspectives as the "carnival" side of democratic living. A carnival is a place that lies outside the established social order (Bakhtin, 1984). It is an occasion where people can let down their social guards, relax, and perhaps even mock the more sedate and somber sides of their lives. Sidorkin (1999) notes that a "democracy . . . needs people not to take it too seriously" and that citizens of democratic societies must always be ready to "challenge, deconstruct, and ridicule . . ." (p. 137). Without this more fluid and nimble approach to life, human interactions can become too weighted down by the rules, rituals, and procedures of hierarchical social structures. To return to a central theme of chapter 1, without moments of intellectual play, the forces of *habit* and *custom* can too easily dominate the power and independence of the human *intellect*.

PRACTICING MULTIPERSPECTIVE INQUIRY

Multiperspective inquiry can be practiced through both inner and outer dialogue. Inner dialogue is conversation with oneself. Sidorkin (1999) uses the term "dialogical integrity" to describe this type of thinking:

> Every voice within me has its own position, and can develop a convincing worldview, if only allowed to express itself. All these voices should be treated with respect; all of them are equally authentic. When I live my life I should never make a final decision about which part of me is right and which part is wrong. I must keep many voices alive and ready for interactions in the context of unique occurrence. Some voices may merge, some whither, and some further split into yet more voices. But if my internal chorus is reduced to just one voice . . . what remains is but a sterile dogma. . . . I need the multiplicity of strong internal voices capable of disagreeing with each other. In fact, I have to cherish these contradictions and inconsistencies, for they are necessary for maintaining my internal dialogue. (p. 44)

External dialogue is conversation with others, and its integrity is based on careful listening and mutual response. There is no external dialogue if the parties involved are talking past one another and/or misrepresenting each other's views. In its extreme version, this type of miscommunication can more accurately be described as parallel monologues between two or more people who happen to be occupying the same space. Burbules (1993) presents three "principles" or "virtues" of honest and sincere dialogue: *participation, commitment,* and *reciprocity.* Participation refers to open and voluntary conversations that enable "any participant . . . to raise topics, pose questions, challenge other points of view, or engage in any of the other activities that define the dialogical interaction" (p. 80). Commitment refers to candid and complete involvement—a "persistent and extensive [communication] across a range of shared concerns, even difficult or divisive ones . . . and [the willingness] to disclose one's underlying reasons, feelings, and motivations, when asked" (p. 81). Finally, reciprocity refers to mutual fair play: "What we ask of others we must be prepared for them to ask of us; and what we expect of others we must expect of ourselves. If we ask others questions, they can ask us questions . . . (p. 82).

INQUIRY SCAFFOLDING

The following questions are designed to support your *multi-perspective inquiries*. You will note that this inquiry scaffolding encourages you to playfully embrace the unique personal expressions and the complex nuances of democratically oriented education.

§ Do I encourage the emergence of unique perspectives? Do I carefully listen to what others are saying and feeling, and do I allow for personal passion and expression?

§ Am I willing to explore the shades of truth in any particular point of view? Can I cultivate a more subtle, multilayered, and nuanced understanding of teaching-learning transactions? How do I understand the multidimensionality of the democracy and education relationship?

§ Can I compare different perspectives in a playful spirit? Can I position myself "in-between" contrasting points of view? Can I then construct more fluid positions based on my immersion in alternative frames of reference?

§ Can I practice multiperspective inquiry as both an honest, open-minded internal dialogue and a sincere, highly committed conversation with others?

FOUR TEACHER-CHARACTERS

Before turning to the concluding teacher narrative of this chapter, a special section has been added on four distinctive teaching styles. We have created four imaginary teacher-characters to assist your multiperspective inquiries, and we do so for three important reasons. First, multiperspective inquiry may be the most challenging form of professional study in this book. Our English word *dialogue* traces back to the Greek concept of *dialogos,* which literally translates as the logic of the "dia"—the "in-between." In terms of this original Greek term, a "dialogical" view of the world is the recognition that human wisdom emerges through a playful encounter with diverse perspectives. But how many of us have been raised this way, and how many of us continue to live in a "monological" world that promotes one point of view, one ideology, one integrated set of beliefs over other possibilities? In terms of multiperspective inquiry, we educators must continually ask ourselves, "How much human misery can ultimately be traced back to a more monological approach to human perceptions and opinions?"

Second, if you have a strong monological background, you may have difficulty getting started with multiperspective inquiry. Working with the teacher-characters may provide the additional impetus you need to engage in this form of professional study. Finally, your current professional learning may not allow for "external" multiperspective inquiry. There are a host of reasons for this unfortunate circumstance, including a lack of time, a lack of trust, a hierarchical political environment, and a preoccupation with institutional procedures. Though you may not be able to address these external constraints, you can still practice an "internal" multiperspective inquiry by creating your own personal conversation with the teacher-characters.

Historically significant educational ideologies have been used to create the four teacher-characters, and a brief overview of this ideological foundation is provided in the Appendix. The teacher-characters represent distinct frames of reference on "good" teaching. They have been created as distinct "monological entities" who are not in dialogue with one another. It is left to you to playfully incorporate their unique perspectives into your own internal and external conversations.

The teacher-characters can be adapted to a variety of inquiry purposes, and this chapter ends with a high school English teacher who worked with these imaginary educators for her own professional development aims. To illustrate how the teacher-characters can be tailored to specific intentions, they will be presented in a particular way. They will first introduce themselves and state their professional beliefs. As each one speaks, you will notice a symbol next to his or her name conveying the essence of his or her ideological perspective.

Johnny Jackson's symbol is the image of an *open book,* which conveys his rationalist orientation.

 For Amy Nelson, the *personal computer* symbol communicates her concern for efficient cognitive processing and information-age achievement.

 Dennis Sage's symbol is a *teacher clasping the hand of a student.* This image stands for his faith in the power of personal relationships in education.

For Silvia Rivera, the *scales of justice* symbol represents her passion for social justice.

Because the teacher-characters have been adapted to serve the purposes of this text, their belief statements will be followed by personal commentaries on **artistic becoming.** The teacher-characters have been created to model this book's understanding of *inquiry artistry.* They all want to continuously grow through sophisticated professional study. All four see themselves as evolving teacher-artists.

Johnny Jackson, High School English Teacher

Teaching Beliefs

I grew up on the South Side of Chicago in the early 1950s. My dad was a school custodian, so our family didn't have a lot of money. Still we took advantage of all of the city's cultural resources. It seems as though every weekend we went to a museum, a play, a special art exhibit, or whatever. I guess my mom was the main motivator for these family outings. She grew up in Alabama, and she had a thirst and passion for education. She made sure I worked hard as a student. I can still see her face the day I told her I had been accepted at the University of Chicago.

I majored in English at the University of Chicago, and I'll never forget one professor who taught a course on James Joyce. Our study of Joyce's (1914/1934) novel *Ulysses* was a revelation to me. I couldn't believe so many ideas could be packed into one book. The juxtaposition of the simple everyday lives of the characters with the **great ideas** of Western civilization (Hutchins, 1952) was stunning to behold and contemplate—and it still is!

I'm chair of the English Department at a highly respected college preparatory magnet school in the Chicago Public School System. I have a master's degree in English literature from UC, and I have often thought about going on for a Ph.D. so that I could teach college students. But, deep down, I realize that my calling is with adolescents. I enjoy turning them on to a vast cultural world they know little about—not because they're not bright enough, but simply because they haven't received the proper exposure. I seem to have my mother's missionary zeal for education—particularly when it comes to the boys. I'm one of the few positive African American role models in their lives. With the help of such creative writers as William Shakespeare and Alice Walker, I can help them discover their potential for a broad and enlightened identity.

Speaking of Shakespeare, I read a speech by Lee Shulman (1989) that, for me, captures the essence of the meaningful academic approach to learning. He describes an English teacher who introduces Shakespeare's *Julius Caesar* through an imaginative activity. The teacher asks students to pretend that they are crew members on the starship *Enterprise* led by the highly respected Captain Kirk. Unfortunately, the captain begins to act strangely, and the crew starts to worry that he will ask them to use the power of the *Enterprise* against the very empire they are sworn to serve. What should the student crew members do? Should they become "revolutionaries" and work to remove Captain Kirk from power, or should they remain "loyalists"? The class discussion raises many feelings. (I know it would for my students because a couple of them have brothers and sisters who are associated with gangs.)

The day after the *Enterprise* discussion, the English teacher tells students that they are going to study a play by Shakespeare that raises many of the same issues they covered yesterday. What an imaginative way to introduce *Julius*

Caesar! Shakespeare describes the human comedies and tragedies that are part of our everyday lives, and this teacher found a way to build a meaningful bridge between this great dramatist and the students' past experiences. That's the kind of teaching to which I aspire. For me, the essence of teaching is helping students with their academic meaning-making.

Artistic Becoming

I am an avid reader. The classic works of Western civilization inspire my professional scholarship. I strongly believe in meditating on the works of Homer, Dante, Voltaire, and Cervantes. My inspirational referents are the great ideas that scaffold our culture. My artistic becoming emerges from this study of the Western canon and from attendance at cultural events. I find theatrical productions stimulating and enjoy modern adaptations of classic texts. During the Gulf War, I saw a provocative performance of *Romeo and Juliet* with cast members costumed in fatigues. I support our local symphony. The music of Mozart allows my mind to wander and my thoughts to be unrestrained. The imagination is freed. Often when I am listening, I find myself thinking fondly of my classroom, students, and school. My head becomes filled with possibilities. I reflect on such questions as these:

- Why should educators in our society be concerned with facilitating students' active meaning-making through the study of classics?

- How can I extend my students' active meaning-making experiences into lifelong habits of cultural study?

- Why is it that I am so inspired by teaching and learning centered on the great ideas of Western civilization? Why am I drawn to this philosophy?

- As an educator in a complex, information-age society with democratic ideals, what is my moral vision? How can modern societies stay in touch with their artistic heritage?

- How can I help parents and other educational stakeholders understand the value of disciplined academic study?

I do not watch much television. Most programming is low-brow nonsense and is therefore useless for my teaching style. Can you remember the most popular television show from ten years ago? Has it had an impact on your life? I am careful not to contaminate my thinking with too much "mental junk food," and I am always on the lookout for solid and enduring cultural nourishment.

When I have the means and opportunity, I like to travel. I will never forget my first visit to the Rodin Museum in Paris. Fresh out of college, the sculpture of the *Thinker* affected me profoundly. Just last summer, I took a group of students with me to Italy. In Florence, we saw Michelangelo's *Prisoner,* the head yet unformed and struggling to free itself from the stone. The room was silent, all of us in awe of the power of the great works of art that surrounded us. I enjoy these educational European tours. Generally speaking, Western Europeans have a high regard for artistic and intellectual pursuits, and they have a deep respect for teachers who encourage this same sort of development in their students.

My commitment to education extends beyond the traditional confines of the classroom. As the school's forensic advisor, I encourage students to join our high school debate team because they will receive an invaluable education in the art of reasoning. Too many of today's students have untidy, undisciplined minds; they operate on the basis of emotional impulses. How can they succeed in life? Most of our social problems result from a lack of self-restraint. Educators must work to rectify this situation.

Learning should be a lifelong pursuit. And I model this belief for my students by taking and talking about Ph.D.-level courses at the university. Primarily, I am enrolled in educational philosophy classes. Did you know that Aristotle was the first philosopher to discuss the nature of syllogistic reasoning? I believe in the value of deductive and inductive logic. How many people can identify valid and invalid syllogisms in an argument? I enjoy such pursuits. I do not think I will ever know all of the answers, nor would I ever want to. I am happy filling my life with books, theater, music, art, ideas, philosophy, and reason. Life should be spent in a quest for great ideas.

Amy Nelson, Elementary School Teacher

Teaching Beliefs

My dad is a successful businessman, and I grew up in an affluent suburb outside of Cleveland. I'm 35 years old. I'm quite proud of my dad's accomplishments, and he has always been a big supporter of mine, too. Like when I won the all-school spelling bee as a fifth grader. My strongest opponent was Bobby Watkins, and he never had a chance! I was the "power speller supreme," and I got a special kick out of beating a boy.

Both of my parents are well-organized, hard-working people, and thanks to them I know how to use my time well. Sometimes I think I get too task oriented, but then I realize that life is short and there's much to accomplish. I'm glad I became an elementary school teacher because I can help the next generation acquire the proper work habits.

I like focused people who have goals in life. Sometimes I think I missed my calling and should have gone into business like my dad. But then I realize that many children today aren't lucky enough to be raised by two hard-working parents. They need someone like me to show them the way. I know this is true because former students have stopped by to thank me for that extra push they got in my class.

I'm currently teaching sixth grade and have a master's degree in educational administration and supervision. My elementary school isn't very big, so our only administrator is the principal. I function as the school's informal assistant principal, for which I get paid extra money. I don't mind the additional responsibilities because I plan to apply for a principalship when there is an opening in my school district. Our school is located in one of the new "professional" suburbs outside Columbus, Ohio. Most of our children's fathers—and some of the mothers—work for the new high-tech firms that are prospering in Columbus. Our students are expected to succeed, and they score very high on all the standardized achievement tests. We are quite proud of this record and have even included an insert in the Sunday paper, highlighting the achievement levels of the students in our school district.

I'm also quite proud of my professional accomplishments. I have gone to innumerable workshops on teacher effectiveness, and I know how to maximize my students' academic achievements. I can talk for hours about performance objectives, advanced organizers, student engagement rates, lesson transitions, and so on.

One of my heroines is Dr. Madeline Hunter. (I should say that I tend to respect all high-achieving women, no matter how different their points of view.) Dr. Hunter has synthesized educational research into very readable instructional principles and procedures. I highly recommend her book *Mastery Teaching* (1982), which will help you inquire into the topic of efficient student learning. Teachers can guide their students' active meaning-making. There are specific ways they can teach for understanding, thereby bridging the gap between their students' unfocused childhood interests and the high-profile, high-performance, problem-solving world of professional life. It is this world that is the hope for a strong America in the future.

Artistic Becoming

I believe that the close examination of one's teaching practice is a very important means of professional scholarship. I constantly examine my daily lesson planning:

- ✎ Did I plan lessons that promoted student inquiry, allowed students to find their own meanings, and encouraged them to make sense of content in thoughtful ways?

- ✎ In what ways am I helping students discover responses, relate their ability to create meaning to other aspects of learning, transfer inquiry to other settings, search for counter evidence, and seek awareness of their own unique thought processes?

- ✎ Did I present meaningful, problem-posing incidents that efficiently sparked student thinking? How did I encourage students to explore multiple solutions through thoughtful engagement with learning?

    ❖   How did I encourage student-student, student-teacher, and/or student-parent collaborative problem-solving ventures in the classroom? Do I believe they contribute to students' active ability to create meaning? How?

    ❖   How might I increase collaborative opportunities? As I monitored students' meaning-making and problem-solving progress, was I observing the quality of collaborative inquiry interactions?

    ❖   What is the best way to assess student's cognitive growth? How might I evaluate collaborative cognitive interactions in my classroom?

I have a rather utopian educational vision, and I want it to be realized for both myself and my students. So I keep a journal in my desk drawer, and at the end of each day, I make a list of ways that I might improve the day's teaching. I always want to better myself and the world that surrounds me.

I am constantly working on my critical thinking skills. Too many people's judgments are muddled. Lipman (1995) writes: "Much of our thinking unrolls impressionistically from association to association, with little concern for either truth or validity . . ." (p. 149). I don't want to be an impressionistic thinker; I don't want my students to be, either. Therefore, I continuously work on our reasoning skills together. I have developed teaching units on thinking skills from many sources. For a sampling of these sources, see Chance's *Thinking in the Classroom: A Survey of Programs* (1986).

I am fully dedicated to my school. So many teachers leave at 3:00, but not me! I serve on numerous committees and am constantly working toward the improvement of our system. I want our school report card to be the highest in the state. I have helped to revise the sixth-grade curriculum, our students' conduct code, and the teachers' faculty handbook. I also serve on the faculty council and am secretary of the district union. This leaves little personal time, but I gather much satisfaction and enjoyment from attendance at local, state, and national professional conferences. I love surrounding myself with people who are as passionate about improving education as I am!

I have a strong religious background. I am a Christian who carefully studies the word of God. I don't broadcast my religion, but I am constantly heartened by the examples of good behavior in the Bible. My sense of becoming is based on these examples. I read selections from the Bible every day with the hope that this study will continuously upgrade my character. I try to be a good model to my students. I want them to be inspired by my daily conduct and understand that the behavioral rules in my classroom have a deep resonance in the life of Christ.

I am happy that more of our country's politicians are discussing such topics as "family values." I commit what little time I have left to campaigning for political candidates who share my beliefs. If people had higher moral standards, many of our social problems would be solved. I am very concerned that too many children are not receiving the proper guidance at home. That's why I work so hard with them and for them.

Dennis Sage, Kindergarten Teacher

Teaching Beliefs

I was raised by an artist mother in the San Francisco Bay area and learned to love the creative process. My mother was a photographer for a local newspaper, but that was just for money. She had to work because my dad left us when I was very young. I'm 28 years old, and I don't have any brothers or sisters. Mom built a darkroom in an old, dilapidated garage behind our house and did all her creative work there. She has won many prizes and had her work published in a variety of magazines and books.

I grew up as a member of a loosely affiliated community of artists. I learned how to paint, sculpt, dance, and play the trumpet. I guess that's why I like kindergarten teaching. You can be creative with the children without worrying too much about a bunch of standardized, bureaucratic expectations.

I've studied the works of the great naturalist John Muir, and I'm an avid backpacker. I believe contemplative inquiry is an important part of a quality life, so I have a quiet story time with my students every day. I wonder sometimes what would have happened to our society if our forebears had decided to learn from Native Americans instead of trying to eradicate them. I enjoy studying people and learning about their idiosyncrasies. I might have become a novelist, but I didn't want to be a starving artist. I've seen too many in California.

Instead, I help my students prepare for the wonderful world of literature. They act out all sorts of dramas that we create together. I am fascinated by the whole language movement, and I deeply believe that teachers should help their students actively construct their own meanings from what they read. I sometimes think I should get a master's degree in reading and become a reading specialist or teach second grade.

I think I have gone to every creativity workshop there is. I just love learning about new ways to turn kids on to their own creativity. Have you read *Artistic Intelligences: Implications for Education* (1990), edited by William Moody? The most important bridge in life is between your everyday self and your innermost self, between your profane and sacred sense of life. I want to help my young students learn to balance these two sides of human nature. I want them to feel special about themselves and their unique talents and experience the constant wonder of discovery.

I work for a rural school district in the western foothills of the Sierra Nevada Mountains. My children come from all types of families. We've got everything from low-income, rural families to affluent, computer-age professionals in our school district. I guess I enjoy the pluralism in this part of California. It doesn't have the hard edge associated with urban diversity. Californians believe in "live and let live." I like that kind of individualism. It can mature into a deep wisdom about life.

One of my favorite educational writers is Max van Manen, who is a professor at the University of Alberta. In 1986, he published a short book entitled *The Tone of Teaching*. In this book, van Manen (1986) describes authentic teaching as follows:

> A real math teacher is a person who embodies math, who lives math, who in a strong sense is math. . . . A real English teacher tends not only to love reading, writing, and carrying

poetry under one arm during coffee break; a real English teacher cannot help but poetize the world—that is, think deeply about human experience through the incantative power of words. (pp. 45–46)

I aspire to be this kind of "real teacher." I applaud teachers who have developed a strong educational presence with their students. They understand the aesthetic side of good teaching.

Artistic Becoming

My approach to professional scholarship is grounded in aesthetic awareness. I continuously reflect on the artistry of my transactions with students, but I do this out of a sense of contemplative or meditative silence. I'm not a strongly analytical or behavioral type of person. To me, the purpose of scholarship is to better understand the aesthetics of teaching-learning transactions. I reflect on my teaching so that I can discern the subtleties of my educational interactions with my students. I often ask myself these questions:

- As a facilitator, how did I confirm each student's multiliterate abilities? Did I continually consider the value of alternative approaches and outcomes? How did I allow for diverse thinking among my students?

- What was the rhythm and pace of my students' inquiry experiences? Did I allow time for relaxation in the classroom? Can I avoid being too conscious of content-coverage issues?

- How aesthetically aware was I of my physical and emotional work environment? How would I describe my sensory awareness while teaching? How did I allow for qualitative and creative responses from my students and from myself?

- How do I express sensitivity to students' needs as they engage in inquiry? Am I carefully observing my students' meaning-making responses, noting any successes or problems? Do I provide support when necessary? How do I share their experiences and empathize with their feelings?

๑   How am I fostering open and honest dialogue with and among my students? How do I reflect on my own caring behavior in the classroom?

๑   How do I actively seek opportunities to talk with students' parents, my colleagues, and other educational stakeholders? In what ways do I openly share my meaning-making lessons and evaluative criteria with students, parents, and other stakeholders? Do I swap inquiry stories with my colleagues? How might I share with colleagues my experience of using inquiry as a tool for teaching students how to actively create meanings?

van Manen (1991) writes beautifully about what it means to be a critically thoughtful teacher, what it means to practice *pedagogical tact,* which he defines as "a mindful orientation in our being and acting with children" (p. 149). He opens his book on pedagogical tact with this poetic evocation: "What is a child? To see a child is to see possibility, someone in the process of becoming" (p. 1).

I recognize myself as also being in the process of becoming, and I share this with my students. They think it's funny that the teacher hasn't finished growing up yet. Yet each day I try to allow for powerful moments of aesthetic learning for all of us. Lee (1993) describes these instances in this insightful way:

> It is a moment of great magnitude because of the transformative insight it affords the individual. It is a memorable learning experience for that person after which he or she is forever changed. It is the moment when Archimedes leaped from his bathtub, crying, "Eureka!" The world is suddenly arranged in a new pattern, with new possibilities. That which was dispersed and separate is gathered together and unified with its own emergent meaning. (p. 77)

I love the "Eureka!" in education. Why can't such moments be an integral part of mathematics learning, or social studies learning? Why can't students have aesthetically powerful experiences in all areas of the curriculum? This is what I contemplate as a teacher. My meditations are on the spirit and the joy of learning.

I consider myself a student of life, still growing, exploring, discovering, and searching for "Eureka!" moments. I enjoy and embrace moments of wonder. I have always felt restricted in the traditional classroom and have resisted taking certain graduate courses, even though the state has mandated that I do so. I much prefer the hands-on learning I can get from community workshops. I can learn so much more from intense personal experience and interaction. I love listening to the stories of others. And I write these down whenever I have the opportunity and share them with an informal writing group that I meet with. I believe strongly in the power of narrative. Every day after lunch, my students and I gather in a circle to tell stories. Why? It simply feels like the right thing to be doing.

I can't say that I spend my life in a library reading educational texts and treatises. I love to read, but I much prefer the work of the romantics and the transcendentalists. I find the natural beauty of Wordsworth's poetry and the revolutionary spirit of Thoreau's essays to be truly exhilarating. The truth inherent in their work inspires my educational spirit and scholarship.

Silvia Rivera, Middle School Social Studies Teacher

Teaching Beliefs

I was born in Puerto Rico in 1961, and my family moved to New York when I was two years old. I have three older brothers and two older sisters. As I was growing up, I observed all their problems adjusting to the United States. My brothers had a hard time finding work. It seems like there was just one barrier after another, and it basically boiled down to one big obstacle: prejudice against people of color. One of my brothers took what he thought was the easy way out by joining a gang and getting involved in drugs. He's now serving time in Attica, and I visit him once a month. This is very painful to do, and I cry every time I have to say goodbye. He was always so kind and gentle to me when I was young.

I have very loving parents, and they have been quite supportive. They both had low-paying jobs, but they sent all of us to the same Catholic elementary school so that we would get a better education while growing up in the Bronx. This was a big financial burden, but they never complained. We spoke Spanish at home, but the nuns made sure that we spoke only English at school and that we never mentioned our Hispanic background. We were treated as Catholic souls who were accidentally born Puerto Ricans.

One nun was special to me. She taught me in sixth grade, and she helped me in many ways. She made me feel important, and she taught me to think freely and question things. As I grew older, her ideas got me thinking about all the inequities inflicted upon women. We have fewer opportunities, are paid less, and are generally less respected than men. We are constantly vulnerable to sexual harassment. I also have questions about the male domination of the Catholic church and the sexist machismo in the Hispanic community. If I raise these topics with my mother, she just shakes her head and wonders where I get such crazy ideas.

Thanks to an aunt, I managed to get my college degree and teaching certificate from Brooklyn College. She was unable to complete her college education, but she did everything she could to make sure I finished mine. She helped me with money and clothes, and she even let me stay with her one difficult year when I couldn't find a decent job. It took me seven years to get through college, and I couldn't have done it without my aunt. I've read that some educational reformers want college students to wait until they have their undergraduate degrees in a subject other than education before pursuing their teaching certificate. Such ideas might be good for the rich, but not for the people I know.

I was certified as an elementary school teacher, but I've always had a keen interest in social studies. I've taken extra graduate courses in history, anthropology, political science, and multicultural education. I'm now a social studies specialist at one of the new middle schools in the New York Public School System.

I love turning kids on to social issues—just like that special nun I had in sixth grade. I emphasize multicultural education in my teaching because I want my students to see the important linkages between their distinctive ethnic heritages and the pluralistic society we are trying to become. Instead of celebrating cultural differences, most Americans hide behind sterile, stereotypical middle-class images of good behavior. I know that this is a complex problem, compounded by our mass media and our politicians. Have you read *The Ideology of Images in Educational Media* (Ellsworth and Whatley, 1990)? Those in power like our cultural stereotypes; it helps them maintain their own status and privileges. Where is their Christian sense of justice? Don't they know that Jesus' mission was with the poor?

I want my students to be critical inquirers, not because it is good to be radical, but because it is good to be fair and compassionate. A democratic society should not have so many barriers. Whenever I talk this way to my parents, they get nervous. They say they know their place in society, but do they? Why can't Hispanics share equally in the fruits of our wonderful land? I believe that teachers should openly confront the power structure in our society, and I want to serve as a bridge to a world with more justice. I get inspired when I go to conferences on diversity in education and when I read such texts as *Empowerment through Multicultural Education* (Sleeter, 1990). Soon I plan to begin a graduate program in multicultural education.

Artistic Becoming

My professional scholarship is informed by my commitment to social liberation. I despise injustice in all its guises, and I would leave teaching if I couldn't fight sociocultural oppression in my work. You may think I'm coming on too strong, but let me explain myself. I am wary of qualitative talk, and there are good historical reasons for my wariness. Do you know any aesthetically developed individuals who are ethically limited? Did you know that many Nazis were liberally educated with refined aesthetic tastes in music, sculpture, and the fine arts? Yet, look at what they did. They practiced genocide with technical sophistication. What social policies result from thinking great ideas, practicing thinking skills, and engaging in aesthetic awareness? I am concerned about my and my students' development as citizens of a democratic society. I want to avoid letting my range of scholarship interests become too narrowly bourgeois and personalized.

A social vision lies at the heart of my critical reflection. Imagine a society where citizens embrace the idea of unity-within-diversity and celebrate democratic, multicultural principles, activities, and institutions. They understand that they must struggle together to actualize an inclusive cultural pluralism; otherwise, their society can never become a great civilization. The educational philosopher Maxine Greene (1988) eloquently evokes the emancipatory spirit inherent in this social vision:

> This is what we shall look for as we move: freedom developed by human beings who have acted to make a space for themselves in the presence of others, human beings become "challengers" ready for alternatives, alternatives that include caring and community. And we shall seek, as we go, implications for emancipatory education conducted by and for those willing to take responsibility for themselves and for each other. We want to discover how to open spaces for persons in the plurality, spaces where they can become different, where they can grow. (p. 56)

When I critically study my teaching, I reflect on such questions as these:

§ How perceptive am I to issues of ethics, diversity, equity, and civility in my classroom? In society at large? As I plan, how might I creatively allow for expressions or explorations of these issues?

§ How do I express my care about issues of diversity, civility, and equity? How do I respond to acts of injustice in my own classroom? In my school? How do I recognize diversity, encourage civility, and promote equity? How do I encourage a more democratic society through my own planning and modeling?

§ How might my own inquiries help to eradicate overt and embedded forms of bias related to gender, race, class, sexual orientation, and other significant human differences?

৯ Are any societal views interfering with how I teach for active meaning-making? Do I sense any ironies or contradictions between what and how I teach as they relate to my beliefs about a pluralistic, democratic society?

৯ How do I question the notion of Eurocentrism in my classroom planning and transactions? How do I draw attention to the relationship between knowledge and power in subject, self, and social learning?

I am currently enrolled at a city college where I take graduate education courses. The passion of my professor and classmates has inspired me to explore the idea of postmodern multiculturalism. Traditional multiculturalism focuses on understanding ethnic and other human differences from the point of view of dominant American middle-class values. An example of this type of multiculturalism is the Walt Disney film *Pocahontas*. The American Indian princess Pocahontas is not portrayed as a young woman in an authentic Native American culture. She is an Indian viewed through the lens of a dominant American corporation's interpretation of beauty and goodness. Imagine the real Pocahontas getting in a time machine that takes her to the present time. What if she understood our current American English and saw the Disney film? How would the real Native American woman react to the cartoon character who is supposed to represent her?

Postmodernism refers to the point of view that there are no universal truths. Postmodernists believe that there are no rational rules that humans can use to "objectively" transcend their many differences. They celebrate human diversity without overtly or tacitly promoting dominant American middle-class values. I am constantly fighting for better multicultural awareness. Whenever I witness acts of oppression in my classroom, school, or community, I become involved. I try to educate students, teachers, and community members by hosting various workshops. I love to share what I am learning in class and at conferences! My passion for social justice and equity continuously inspires my teaching actions. Together my students and I engage in a variety of activities, promoting community and cultural awareness and involvement. I recognize my own artistic becoming as being a product of this civic commitment. Each campaign I lead, organization I chair, council I serve, or workshop I host helps me to more fully realize the educator and person I want to be. I enthusiastically share this passion of becoming with my students. I want them to understand what animates my contemplations, and I want them to begin to explore their own social values and visions.

TEACHER-CHARACTER CONCLUSION

You have now been introduced to four imaginary teachers, who are all working on their professional artistry. You have become familiar with their teaching beliefs and their sense of continuing professional growth. Their ideological differences are summarized in Table 3.1. Hopefully, their contrasting perspectives will help you to critically examine your own beliefs about teaching and your own understanding of artistic becoming.

Now that you have been introduced to the teacher-characters, consider these additional *multiperspective inquiry* questions:

§   What is your life story?

§   What experiences have helped to shape you as a teacher?

§   What instances have contributed to your beliefs about "good" teaching for democratic living?

§   If you haven't as yet constructed such beliefs, which teacher-character perspective seems most attractive? Why?

§   How do you lead a life of seeking truth and continuing growth?

§   In what ways are you a teacher-artist?

§   How do you express and celebrate you own artistic becoming?

Though there are no right or wrong answers to these inquiries, teachers can certainly be more or less committed to the critical examination of their professional artistry. Even though the four teacher-characters differ in their orientations, they all set a high personal standard for continuing growth. Hopefully, you will set a similar high standard for yourself.

Table 3.1

Teacher-Artist	Ideological Tradition	Artistic Becoming	Symbol
Johnny Jackson	Academic rationalism	Classical study, cultural appreciation, and contemplative growth	Open book
Amy Nelson	Social efficiency	School reform, cognitive development, and goal-oriented growth	Personal computer
Dennis Sage	Creative developmentalism	Intuition, personal experience, and spiritual and aesthetic growth	Clasped hands
Silvia Rivera	Social reconstructionism	Multicultural advancement, civic commitment, and critical growth	Scales of justice

Teacher Narrative*

I have always heard voices.

I am smiling as I write this first sentence, smiling at your imagining a teacher who spends her mornings and afternoons talking to her many selves. Really, it's not so bad. In fact, I embrace the many aspects of my self, reveling in the differences and complexities that somehow amass into a mixture called "me." Some choose to silence these many faces, facets, and forms, in favor of "the

---

*Contributed by Mary Styslinger.

one." Some select the "all-knowing" teaching personality sure to stimulate thought with students and promote harmony with colleagues. But not me. For I have learned to embrace "the many."

I began to hear the voices when I was a child. Growing up in Birmingham, Alabama, the daughter of upper-class parents who loved and cared for me, I was one of the privileged. My high school was not plagued by poverty or problems, and I was provided with the many educational opportunities that come with privilege. I played the piano. No voices then. I cheered at football games. No voices then. I went out with my friends. The voices were faint. I acted in plays. The voices grew louder. I questioned in class. The voices screamed.

My friends were many and diverse. Although I had access to the privileged "Heathers" at my school, I chose to associate with whomever I found interesting and stimulating. Often, this was not the popular clique. Stephan fascinated me. His mother was French, and his hair fell forward in a way that reminded me of Simon LeBon, lead singer of the British rock group Duran Duran. We would whisper to one another in algebra class, sharing confidences we felt sure would shock our teachers and friends. He was gay; I was accepting. Elif was from Turkey; she was different, not being of "Anglo-Saxon" heritage or Protestant. Her eyes were pools of ink, a direct contrast to the frantic giggles that could burst from her at the most inopportune moments. Usually during English class. Farran was a Regency beauty—brilliant and fair; her wealth of intellect and lack of tan led to her graduating without a single date in high school. Stuart, having recently moved from Scotland, was the coolest. A member of the stage crew, he once pounded out a dent in my parents' Pontiac after I banged into a cement pole at a mall parking garage. Robin was the perfect homecoming queen; her father had a white Corvette with T-tops, and in it we partied and smoked to Van Halen tunes. Jeff was the love of my adolescent life. President of both the Student Government Association and the Federation of Christian Athletes, he made my heart and body ache with wanting.

My friends were a motley crew. Much like a chameleon, I was able to switch colors and cliques. Although loyal to all, I was limited to no "one." Instead, I delighted in the differences of complexions, orientations, personalities, interests, and backgrounds offered me. My world was filling with perspectives—with colors and sounds before unknown. I observed. I listened.

I wanted to act. Knowing I had a natural penchant for role-playing, I auditioned for the school musical. I didn't make it. I wasn't a very good singer. So I auditioned for the school play. I made it. Thus began my life-long relationship with the theater. My passion for drama has lasted longer than any friend or lover. It has remained by my side throughout my educational and teaching career; it has been a constant companion as I have relocated and strived for professional and personal growth. It has encouraged, developed, and refined the many voices.

For an actor must embrace duality. Even at the tender age of fourteen, I knew I must lose myself in and with an "other." A stranger had to become as familiar to me as my self. She had to become part of me. I had to analyze the internal dimensions of a character—her background, emotions, values, beliefs, and ideas. Then I would question how she was similar or different from me. What did she want? What did I want? The external dimensions of character asked me to consider our postures, movements, gestures, mannerisms, voices, and dress. In what ways were we similar or different? In order to create believable characters, an actor must be highly introspective. He or she must come to question and know his or her self in powerful and profound ways. He or she must also acutely study the world that surrounds.

What we do not find within ourselves, we find in others. What an actor does not know, he or she has to imagine, then bring into being. Much like an artist, we re-create borrowed images. Only the actor's creations must do more than just be seen—they must speak, move, hear, touch, smell, taste, and feel. A heightened perception leads us to discovery. We remember the sound that voices make when people are exhausted, observe the way that an elderly woman scuffles along the sidewalk, listen to the crunching sound in our mouths, feel the way that the carpet tickles against our toes, inhale the scents that linger after a fall bonfire, relish the flavors that assault our tongue, and empathize with the sufferings and joys that life brings to us all.

My love affair with acting led to my love affair with difference. As I became more sensitive to the sensual world that surrounded me, I grew ever more accepting of particularity and peculiarity. An actor simply cannot afford to be judgmental. If he or she is to make a character real, he or she must fully accept those aspects and dimensions necessary for character development. Although many times those borrowed dimensions of character were unlike me, I welcomed the diverse traits. And as time passed, in lieu of becoming an elitist, I found myself, much to my parents' chagrin, tolerant and accepting of varied races, genders, personalities, religions, and orientations. I began to hear things that sometimes my family, friends, teachers, and community did not.

As I sat in my perfect high school, in my perfect suburb, wearing my Guess jeans, listening to a lecture on *The Scarlet Letter*, I started to talk with myself. Everybody else was silent. Everybody else was listening and taking notes. I simply had to speak with someone. So I did so in my head. I began to question whether or not I would have taunted Hester, were I a Puritan. I bet I would have. Then I began to wonder about the nature of the relationship between Hester and Dimmesdale. They had sex. If I were Hester, would I have fallen in love with such a wimp? What was it like to kiss a clergyman? Mrs. Carter, our next-door neighbor, was married to a preacher; they had a huge house with white columns. If I were Dimmesdale, I would have wanted Hester—the forbidden fruit. Why are humans so drawn to the forbidden? Then, I became Pearl, the love child. Why wouldn't my father acknowledge me? There must be something wrong with me. I was startled out of my reverie by the bell.

I remember that moment as if it happened yesterday. Although Mrs. Quinn's monological voice was droning on and on and on in that classroom, I had chosen to listen to the many inside my head. One perspective was no longer sufficient. I began to question. I started a tiny revolution.

The following day, I returned to class, this time wearing my "Calvins." I was determined to shake things up. "Mrs. Quinn," I asked, "did you ever wonder if the Puritans were rather like the Baptists?" Silence. I tried to explain. "I mean, don't we judge people—you know, the ones who aren't saved—harshly too?" Here was a student, desperately trying to make sense of a dry text, striving for some sort of personal insight. I waited.

"Mary, this book is set in seventeenth-century Boston; I really don't think it's necessary to draw similarities with ourselves," Mrs. Quinn finally answered. It was a safe answer. A few seconds passed.

"Y'all know," Joe's southern drawl was thick, "I was kinda thinkin' that maybe life weren't so bad back then . . . simpler—not havin' to think fer yourself that much. People jest did what they were toled."

I was excited and couldn't wait to reply, "But how much thinking do we really do for ourselves now? Like, did you ever wonder if there is any villain in this novel at all?"

Mrs. Quinn decided to play along. Good for her. "The most evil character would have to be Chillingworth since he is taking revenge in insidious ways."

"But he's hurt," I cried, "he's wounded by Hester's betrayal, by love! Honestly, everyone seems just as evil to me. Hester should take off that stupid letter by now and get over it! She seems to be milking it for all it's worth. And Dimmesdale is so weak he makes me puke. He hurts everyone because he can't stand up and do what's right. And Pearl needs a good whippin'," my own drawl always became more obvious when I got excited.

Now we were getting somewhere. I wanted this conversation to go on and on and on. There was a desperate need in this classroom for some critical thinking and playful conversation. I wanted to know more of what Joe thought, of what Tammy thought, of what Bo thought. Instead of having a conversation with myself, I wanted to have one with those who looked, thought, felt, and spoke differently from me. I wanted to move the inner dialogue outward.

Mrs. Quinn's voice resonated throughout the room, talking past and over the classroom chatter, which was just starting to sputter and gain momentum. "This was a very interesting discussion," she began, her eyes betraying her true feelings, "but if I don't finish talking about the many examples of symbolism and imagery in this book, then you will have to finish that up for homework tonight." Silence.

I think back upon those final words and cringe. As a teacher, I know what an opportunity was lost in that classroom. How many unique and varied perspectives might have come to light on that very day if she had only allowed for and responded to our passion and expression. What multiple meanings might have revealed themselves through dialogue with one another? Mrs. Quinn was too frightened by the possibilities. So instead, there was silence.

Soon it was time to leave the thriving metropolis of Birmingham for the academic plains of Auburn University. Determined to find and create a place where students could share perspectives and grow from encounters with one another, I enrolled in the education department and began my study of English. During my undergraduate, but even more so in my graduate classes, I was able to play with a variety of perspectives. Seated in a semicircle, our professor perched on the desk with glasses tottering on the bridge of her nose, we would debate the happenings in Gilman's "The Yellow Wallpaper" or Poe's "The Fall of the House of Usher." There were no "right" or "exact" answers to be given—only a variety of interpretations upheld with textual support. Was the narrator in an insane asylum as most of the males argued, or was she being driven crazy in her own home by an unfaithful husband as we females tended to maintain? Did the Usher house really crumble in the end, or was it a metaphorical representation of a crumbling mind? The debates grew heated and discussions animated, so much so that they were often continued after class at Greeley's, a local watering hole. I was in heaven.

As is typical of English majors, I eventually began my study of contemporary literary criticism and theory with essays from the modernist and formalist movements. I delved into criticism from six major paradigms or large systems of thought—rhetorical, structuralist, poststructuralist, psychological, historical, and gender-based. I explored. I interrogated. This was no scientific or objective study. The interplay of critic and text devoured me. No choices were being made. For I did not want to become a member of "one" critical school. Instead, I attended "the many," gaining insight into each critical system. "Doing" criticism became one of the most important things I, as a literate person, could do. It was nourishment, essential for my intellectual and personal growth. Reading, understanding, and learning all became related to this "doing." Never would I approach a text or life in the same way.

If a singular literary work could be viewed from a variety of perspectives, so could almost anything! My world became more complex and complicated. I could see two, three, four, five, six sides to everything! I embraced the nuance. I accepted that there was no absolute, no singular "truth" and opted for the alternative of contrasting frames of reference. I finally understood what the voices had been whispering and urging all along.

Upon graduation, I carried this belief into my first classroom. I looked around and saw many rows and no windows. Like numerous first-year teachers, I was given the room that was left over. Oh well, at least I had a room, I smiled to myself, knowing friends who would be "traveling" their first year. I studied this room closely for a reason. I knew that if I wanted a safe place for dialogue and difference, then I would have to create an environment that was conducive to such. The arrangement of desks did matter. But the room was so small! How was I ever going to create a circular or collaborative desk arrangement in this place? I pondered. Eventually, I settled on horizontal rows, directly facing one another. This left me space to move around in between and an almost stage-like area between the two blocks of seats.

Next, I looked at the walls. I honestly believe that there is a shade of sickly yellow that is provided free of charge to all schools and hospitals. Yuck. I needed posters, lots of them. But I was broke. I bought some wrapping paper that had colored books printed all over it from a discount store. Then I proceeded to wrap my walls with it—it hung at angles—and on the paper I had quotes—quotes about censorship, quotes from works we would be reading, quotes that led to thought and introspection. No kittens hanging from a rope in this room. I left a large space for student work to be displayed, swept, and went home.

In the three days I had before the faculty meetings began, I scoped my assigned text and sighed. I would need to do a lot of copying this year. But again, I was happy that I had enough books, knowing friends who didn't. If I wanted sincere inquiry and dialogue in my classroom, then I had to provide students with reading assignments that would prod their higher level thinking. I needed literature that would provoke and stimulate thought and conversation. I found it.

But most, I knew, would depend on myself. How I interacted with my students, the questions I asked, the responses I gave, would decide how many chances they would be willing to take in my classroom. And there were the assignments and tests I would design. Would I be one of those teachers who claimed to be a constructivist educator, encouraging reader response and meaning-making from students during class discussion, then handing out objective tests and scantron sheets every Friday? I hoped not.

Certainly not every day or lesson was perfect during those first years of teaching, but at least I tried. We began with a review of literal happenings, but spent the majority of class time building, scaffolding, from there. Students were given opportunities and were encouraged to share their personal reactions to the literature in groups, in journals, and in essays. Projects and activities were planned that nurtured students' voices and styles. Opportunities for sharing were plentiful. My role became one of facilitating, moderating, and promoting an environment that was accepting of various student responses. This was not always easy, but the results were well worth the effort.

I specifically remember teaching a poetry unit. We started with music. I asked my students to bring in lyrics that they found really meaningful. In small groups, they listened to each other's songs and tried to interpret the lyrics together. Then they presented their own discoveries to the class. It certainly would have been faster to just define poetical terms and take a test on them, but my students would have missed the opportunity of listening to music and formulating their own interpretations. Sure, I did introduce poetry terms, but I did it later instead of sooner.

After each group presented the results of their inquiry learning, I then provided the terms and a problem—let's try to figure out what these words mean together. For the next few days, we analyzed poetry—some poems I brought in; other poems they brought in. There were no "right" meanings; there were only interpretations and support for them. All along, when inspired, we wrote poetry of our own. Then, on the last day, we lit candles, dressed up, shared coffeehouse snacks, and read our poems. I even read a few of my own.

I taught for ten years in two schools—one private, the other public. Along the way, though, I realized that I was still hungry. Not only did I want to facilitate dialogue among my own students, I wanted to be part of the student dialogue once again. I wanted to feed on new ideas, new theories, new methods, and share these with others. I wanted to add new voices to the growing chorus. So I enrolled in the doctoral program at Kent State University.

In my curriculum and instruction courses, I was encouraged to reflect in ways that would lead to transformative teaching and professional leadership. I was introduced to four teacher-characters who represented four distinct teaching styles, drawn from historically significant educational ideologies. Academic rationalism was embodied by Johnny Jackson, social efficiency by Amy Nelson, creative developmentalism by Dennis Sage, and social reconstructionism by Silvia Rivera. I liked these characters. For many of them were familiar to me.

Johnny reminded me of a colleague, Mr. Jones. He was the smartest teacher I knew—he fostered in his students a love and appreciation for knowledge. His presence and bearing were strong, and his expectations were high, yet kids were drawn to him. Amy was everywhere. She especially reminded me of a good friend of mine, Patti Frazier. Patti, I swear, served on every committee there was—she lived for North Central Evaluations. Every time I walked by her classroom, I was amazed—her students would be busy reading independently, designing projects, or writing in journals. This woman and her students were so industrious! I respected that. Dennis was Mark. Mark wanted his students to enjoy reading and writing—an objective not often held by secondary English teachers. He prided himself on being called the only "elementary" teacher at the high school. He was passionate about his students' creative abilities. Silvia was embodied by Beckie. A new teacher, her passion was a source of inspiration to us all. She had her kids problem solving in the community, writing letters to the editor, collecting canned foods for the needy, volunteering to give blood for banks, and recycling paper from the teacher's workroom. What a teacher!

The teacher-characters were so very real to me. I saw them embodied, walking and talking in the hallways at my school. I respected their diverse teaching styles. But I also began to question my own sense of self and style within these educational, ideological manifestations. Who was I? Where did I fit in?

I decided I needed to read a bit more. So I checked out Bernier and Williams' (1973) *Beyond Beliefs: Ideological Foundations of American Education.* In this text, the authors offer six major belief systems, which, they argue, give direction to education in the United States: scientism, romanticism, puritanism, progressivism, nationalism, and educationism. (For more on these six ideologies, see the Appendix.) The scientist orders reality, implies predictability, needs logic, accepts probability, demands neutrality, and controls the environment. The romantic exposes uniqueness, embraces imagination, possesses rebellion, rejects restrictions, emphasizes subjective feelings and intuitions, and thirsts for individuality. The puritan encourages morality, struggles against sin, restricts freedom, demands excellence, sometimes dictates, and disallows permissive attitudes. The progressive possesses faith in the future, relates well to technological advancement, believes change can be controlled, desires improvements in institutions, advocates involvement in child-related problems, and expresses concern for the disadvantaged. The nationalist refers to nation-state, preserves national integrity, sustains cultural solidarity, seeks political autonomy, develops loyal citizens, and creates feelings of solidarity. The educationist sees relationship between school and society, seeks to incorporate extracurricular activities into the curriculum, functions to legitimize and perpetuate schooling, preserves society through formal education, implies education is improved through formalism, and recognizes schooling as creating work for children.

Although I found the reading stimulating, it didn't seem to help much. For I could still see human representations of these belief systems in the faculty lounge and at department meetings. They were still recognizable faces to me, even more so since my reading. I, however, was a big blur. I was fuzzy. How then was I ever going to complete the assignment given me by an overzealous professor: critically examine a constructivist practice and create a paper or product of your inquiry. How could I critically examine my poetry unit from a perspective if I wasn't even sure which perspective I held?

After all, I was Johnny, Dennis, Amy, *and* Silvia. I was part scientist, part romantic, part puritan, part progressive, part nationalist, and part educationist. I could see the value in **all** of the belief systems. Sometimes I was scientific in my approach with students, believing that behavior could and often should be modified. Sometimes I was the romantic, nurturing spontaneity, authenticity, and individuality in my students. I was the puritan as I tried to approach moralistic messages in texts. My passion for solidarity in the classroom exposed my sense of nationalism. I, the progressive, often stressed relativity, moderation, and reflection. And my belief in education as contributing to social cohesion revealed my educationist ideology.

My classroom was a place where varying styles, voices, theories, practices, and philosophies were celebrated. The reason I was having such difficulty with this assignment was because I was trying to accept, embody, and limit my self to only one perspective, when, instead, my inquiry should be dialogical and multiperspective! I embraced this "Eureka!" moment in my own life's education. I was not "one." Instead, I was "in between."

I embraced the process of multiperspective inquiry. My poetry unit sat before me on the desk, and I began to analyze it from the mindset of the scientist, the romantic, the puritan, the nationalist, the progressive, and the educationist. The voices were loud. They questioned, probed, and critiqued:

Nationalist: I would like to see this teacher concentrate more on developing loyal citizens somehow. Now, that poem "Chicago" by Sandburg expresses cultural solidarity and homogeneity.
Romantic: I hate homogeneity!
Nationalist: Why aren't you including any poetry by Francis Scott Key? Now there was a great poet.
Scientist: How can you prove that? This is why I hate poetry.
Romantic: I'll say it again—do what you want!

Puritan: No, you should do what is right.

Educationist: Excuse me, but does your unit plan correspond with the course of study you were given by the institution?

Progressive: You should only care about that if it's relevant to the child. But aren't there some computer programs that could help make poetry more interesting for you and your students?

The dialogue was playful as no "one" voice overpowered another. But how was I going to represent this inquiry process to my professor? Although I was deeply engaged and involved with the varied perspectives, it seemed a shame to present this dialogue as a traditional research report.

My multiperspective inquiry experience took many forms, representing, once again, my resistance to the "singular." In an effort to explore my own multiple intelligences, I created a spatial project, an intrapersonal project, a linguistic project, a logical-mathematical project, and an interpersonal project.

First, the internal dialogue became external and manifested itself in the form of a video (spatial). I directly faced the camera as varied voices and typesettings confronted me with questions. I looked upward to answer the puritan, up right to answer the progressive, right to answer the romantic, down to answer the nationalist, up left to answer the educationist, and left to answer the scientist. It was a dizzying experience.

I recorded a monologue (intrapersonal intelligence), which revealed and shared discoveries made and feelings acknowledged along the inquiry way. Then I wrote a poem (linguistic intelligence), which exemplified these discoveries and feelings:

The Highwire

On a highwire,
Like an acrobat I balance.
Sometimes juggling:
moralize politicize
industrialize technologize
analyze institutionalize
Trying to stuff six ideologies into a volkswagen.
But the teacher cannot be contained.
Scientific whips are handled,
Romantic roars are unleashed—
A battle for domination.

Sometimes a sideshow
For the peanut-crunching crowd,
Who enjoy the dual face—
Mostly rebellious
Mostly logical,
The face of a clown.

I demonstrated my inquiry through a chart (logical-mathemati-cal intelligence, Table 3.2).

Finally, I demonstrated my interpersonal intelligence through inter-viewing and transcribing conversations held with colleagues about their own ideologies as demonstrated in their teaching of poetry. I was then satisfied. I was not "one." I was "many." And the product of my thinking was not "singular." It, too, was "many."

Life, for me, has been filled with varying perspectives. My personal relationships, theatrical experiences, academic efforts, classroom discussions, and student interactions have been strengthened through my multiperspective inquiries. My personal and professional self continues to grow and evolve with each new voice I hear. So I keep listening, recognizing myself, like Johnny, Amy, Dennis, and Silvia, as being in the continual process of "artistic becoming."

REFERENCES

Bakhtin, M. (1984). *Problems of Dostoevsky's poetics* (C. Emerson, Ed. & Trans.). Minneapolis: University of Minnesota Press.

Bernier, N. R., & Williams, J. E. (1973). *Beyond beliefs: Ideological foundations of American education.* Upper Saddle River, NJ: Prentice Hall.

Burbules, N. C. (1993). *Dialogue in teaching: Theory and practice.* New York: Teachers College Press.

Chance, P. (1986). *Thinking in the classroom: A survey of programs.* New York: Teachers College Press.

Ellsworth, E., & Whatley, M. (Eds.). (1990). *The ideology of images in educational media.* New York: Teachers College Press.

Table 3.2

	Scientism	Romanticism	Puritanism	Nationalism	Progressivism	Educationism
Order	X		X			X
Unity	X		X	X		X
Reason	X				X	X
Technology	X				X	X
Control	X		X	X	X	X
Morality			X		X	X
Individuality		X				X
Intuition		X				
Homogeneity	X		X	X		X
Self-expression		X		X		
Goodness of man		X		X	X	
Subjectivity		X				
Risks		X				
Freedom		X		X		
Perfection	X		X		X	X
Political			X	X		X
Cultural					X	X
Loyalty			X	X		X
Progress	X				X	
Reflection	X		X	X	X	
Creativity		X				
Institutionalism	X		X		X	X
Society			X	X	X	X

Gallagher, S. (1992). *Hermeneutics and education*. Albany, NY: State University of New York Press.

Greene, M. (1986). In search of critical pedagogy. *Harvard Educational Review, 56* (4), 427–441.

Greene, M. (1988). *The dialectic of freedom*. New York: Teachers College Press.

Hunter, M. (1982). *Mastery teaching*. El Secundo, CA: TIP Publications.

Hutchins, R. M. (1952). *Great Books of the Western World: Vol. 1. The great conversation: The substance of a liberal education* (pp. 1–131). Chicago: Encyclopaedia Britannica.

Joyce, J. (1934). *Ulysses*. New York: Random House. (Original work published 1914)

Lee, K. (1993). Transcendence as an aesthetic concept: Implications for curriculum. *The Journal of Aesthetic Education, 27* (1), 75–82.

Lipman, M. (1995). Critical thinking—What can it be? In A. C. Ornstein & L. S. Behar (Eds.), *Contemporary issues in curriculum* (pp. 145–152). Boston: Allyn & Bacon.

Moody, W. (Ed.). (1990). *Artistic intelligences: Implications for education*. New York: Teachers College Press.

Noddings, N. (1984). *Caring: A feminine approach to ethics and moral education*. Berkeley, CA: University of California Press.

Pinar, W. F., Reynolds, W. M., Slattery, P., & Taubman, P. M. (1995). *Understanding curriculum: An introduction to the study of historical and contemporary curriculum discourses*. New York: Peter Lang.

Shulman, L. S. (1989, January). *Aristotle had it right: On knowledge and pedagogy*. Keynote address at the Annual National Meeting of the Holmes Group. Washington, DC.

Sidorkin, A. M. (1999). *Beyond discourse: Education, the self, and dialogue*. Albany, NY: State University of New York Press.

Sleeter, C. (Ed.). (1990). *Empowerment through multicultural education*. Albany, NY: State University of New York Press.

van Manen, M. (1986). *The tone of teaching*. Richmond Hill, Ontario: Scholastic-TAB.

van Manen, M. (1991). *The tact of teaching: The meaning of pedagogical thoughtfulness*. Albany, NY: State University of New York Press.

CHAPTER 4

DELIBERATIVE INQUIRY

§

On the first day of summer vacation, Sarah Davis rolled out of bed during what would have been her third-period geometry class. She was looking forward to a break from the fast pace of grading tests, making up math lesson plans, and coaching the girls' tennis team. She felt like she never had enough time to think during the school year. But not this morning; she was going to take a long walk with her dog and think about her summer plans.

However, by the time Sarah reached the bottom of the driveway, she was already thinking about her teaching assignment for next year. In addition to her usual schedule, she was to teach a new course entitled "Study Skills for Math." Students enrolled in this course would be upperclassmen who had yet to pass the math portion of the state proficiency test that all students must pass to graduate from high school. Even though Sarah disagreed with teaching to a test, the administration and parents were clamoring for higher test scores. Her setting was out of her control.

Anxiety swept over Sarah. She had never taught a class like this before. Many thoughts raced through her head. "How do I motivate students who have had little or no success in previous math courses? Will a lack of motivation increase the number of discipline problems? What should I teach when there will be a wide range of math backgrounds present? Do I teach a few topics in depth so that they understand the material or cover more topics in less depth? Will I have time to allow them to work in groups and construct their own meanings of a topic?"

Then, Sarah suddenly stopped. She realized that her thoughts were not being productive or generative. "I am only looking at how this course affects *me.* My fears concerning how to teach the course made me overlook how the course will be perceived by the most important people: **my students.** They are probably stressed about taking another math course that they feel they will really struggle with as they have in the past. They probably want to know what this course and the proficiency test have to do with real life. What happens if they do not pass the math portion of the test again; will they be more likely to drop out of school? This is the concern of administrators and parents. If I really care about my students, then I should put their feelings and attitudes first."

Sarah slowed down her walking speed and deliberately contemplated what she was going to do in the course next school year. She figured that she first needed to define the problem that she was facing. After weighing her concerns with those of her students and the community, she concluded that she wanted to create a learning environment where the students truly understood, not just memorized, the math content that they wrestled with in class. Focusing her thoughts on this problem made the situation seem less overwhelming.

Coming up with solutions to this problem was a challenge that Sarah wanted to take on. She reflected on math classes where her students developed a strong sense of pride in what they learned and workshops that she attended where other teachers tackled similar problems with success. She came up with a lot of good ideas and played around with them in her head for the next twenty minutes.

Sarah felt the need to bounce some ideas off of others. She thought about who she could talk to. "Gail and Ben have taught classes with students with weak math backgrounds; they could provide some excellent insights. And why not talk to some students who have taken remedial classes before? Maybe the curriculum director for the school district could give me some materials such as manipulatives and activities that can supplement the textbook. Perhaps I could arrange a meeting with all of these people to discuss the course and its impact on the students. I'm sure they would agree to it because we all care about the students and the actions that are taken to resolve this problem."

When Sarah arrived home, she could not wait until her walk tomorrow so that she could think of more solutions to her problem and think of related problems that may stem from her possible solutions. She was now really looking forward to next year to enact some of her solutions and revise her plan of action. In particular, inquiring into the

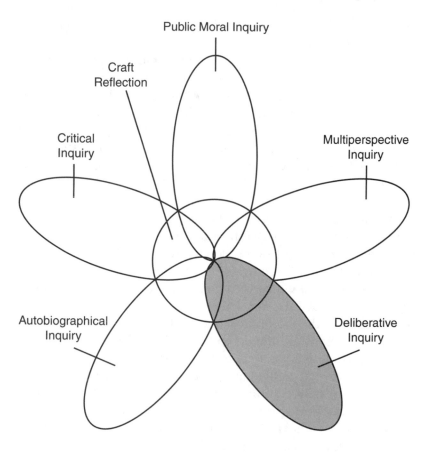

Public Moral Inquiry

Craft
Reflection

Critical
Inquiry

Multiperspective
Inquiry

Autobiographical
Inquiry

Deliberative
Inquiry

problem from the students' perspectives opened her eyes and allowed her to envision many more possible solutions. She realized that she liked deliberating with the "big picture" in mind.

INTRODUCTION

In attempting to address a problem that means a lot to her, Sarah asks many questions, which leads to more questions. At the end, she does not appear to be any better off than when she started. In fact, through questioning she has gained valuable insights by walking in the shoes of others who are directly or indirectly tied to her inquiry. This careful examination of a problem from several points of view in order to decide on a course of action is one aspect of individual and group deliberations. We will use the term *disciplined inquiry* to describe this form of disciplined professional study.

This chapter will describe how deliberations can be a powerful way to express your care for others and push you in new directions of growth as a teacher. Although we hear this word in our everyday language, such as in the phrase "jury deliberations," the term is not a common one in today's schools. In the following discussion, we will see how group deliberations, as well as deliberating with oneself, can open our eyes to new ways of looking at the teaching and learning problems that we encounter.

According to Webster's (1996) dictionary, deliberation is the "consideration and discussion of alternatives before reaching a decision; the quality of being deliberate; carefulness; slowness" (p. 527). In the field of curriculum studies, scholars are continually defining what it means to deliberate in educational settings (McCutcheon, 1995; Harris, 1986; Schwab, 1978). What is missing in the preceding definition and in the literature, however, is how deliberations are linked to teaching for democratic living, and this linkage will be a central concern of this chapter.

To ensure that individuals take multiple perspectives into account when deliberating, Schwab (1978) suggests looking at curriculum questions from the four commonplaces of *student, teacher, subject,* and *milieu,* which we will refer to as the *setting.* He believes that looking at educational problems through these four lenses allows us to see things that we could not see from one vantage point alone. Figure 4.1 shows these four positions in the form of puzzle pieces. The puzzle is the problem that an individual or group is trying to solve.

Depending on the problem and its context, an individual or group may emphasize one or two commonplaces that are particularly relevant. Therefore, a piece of the puzzle may be bigger than others, such as the student piece, or a piece may not need to be considered, such as the subject piece. For example, read the following questions and think about which of the four positions are the most and least integral to the problem.

§   How do I stop a handful of my students from picking on John?

§   How do I help my students appreciate the aesthetics of poetry?

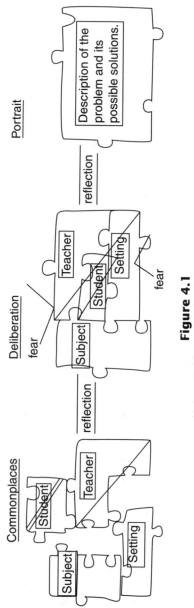

Figure 4.1
Using Deliberation to Solve a Problem

❧ How can I help rectify the fact that there are a lower percentage of African American students in my advanced-placement physics course relative to white students?

❧ How can I express my belief in portfolio assessment and use this method of evaluation when many parents of my students are against the idea?

A goal of the deliberation process is to describe the problem and suggest possible solutions. Before this occurs, however, an individual or each member of a group must reflect on how he or she perceives the student, teacher, subject, and setting pieces and the relationships between each of them. For example, let's look at the poetry question. In terms of each piece of the puzzle, a teacher may ask himself or herself a series of questions. What poems will stimulate my students' thinking and make poetry relevant to them? How can I present the poems in such a way that the students construct their own meaning of them? What poetry can encourage aesthetic experiences? Will my colleagues who focus solely on the grammar and structure of poems in their teaching support my endeavor?

Although these questions respectively address each commonplace (student, teacher, subject, and setting), we can see that there is some overlapping. The issue of teacher presentation makes no sense without taking students into consideration, and the subject (poetry) plays a role in the setting issue. There are no clear-cut boundaries separating the commonplaces. This is why the pieces are more meaningful when they are put together during the deliberation process.

A deliberation is a journey where an infinite number of questions and perspectives can be raised in each commonplace. Engaging in a deliberation on your own is difficult because you have to come up with all of these questions and imagine the viewpoints of students, colleagues, parents, and others who are directly or indirectly linked to the problem. You may encounter conflicting interpretations of the problem, and it may be only through a playful consideration of contrasting perspectives (see chapter 3) that you'll be able to find the best fit of the individual "pieces," that is, the best solution to a particular problem. Imagining what other people think is a big task, which is why group deliberations are a welcome alternative. Getting others to freely share their ideas is not easy, however, because they may be afraid of their views being attacked, as in a debate, or they may feel that their ideas are not "good enough." How do we get people to feel confident in their perspectives and thoughts so that they do not feel threatened and run away from this opportunity to grow? Deliberations need to occur in a caring environment that will minimize the possibility of fear and defensiveness.

This approach to solving problems is most successful when it is enacted by people who care about the problem. Agnes (1999) describes a caring individual as someone who is "other-oriented." She elaborates further on the essence of caring:

> Caring has been described as trusting, accepting, friendly, respectful, flexible, democratic, nonpunitive, nonmoralistic, self-disciplined and other-empowering. . . . That is, people who care usually believe that they are personally capable of attending to another and making a difference. They choose to depend on themselves and on their own initiatives to solve problems in these efforts, rather than rely mainly upon others. (p. 172)

Teachers who address problems that they encounter in their classroom or school and generate possible solutions from various perspectives, either on their own or in discussion with others, are truly caring.

Caring educators, parents, students, and others who engage in a group deliberation encourage dialogue that embraces multiple perspectives. They are empathetic to each others' point of view. Noddings (1984) points out that "the purpose of dialogue is to come into contact with ideas and to understand, to meet the other and to care" (p. 186). Participants actively listen to ideas, not just hear them. They respond to others' thoughts in generative ways, where both the listeners and speakers exchange perspectives without demeaning them. Everyone wants to grow in his or her thinking. To do this, trust must be built among participants so that fear can be cast aside. Through caring deliberations, people make use of their intellect for generous and generative purposes. We could say that their deliberative inquiries are guided by the second and third principles of *democratic living,* as discussed in chapter 1.

The first principle of *democratic living,* that moral conduct is best practiced through *intellect* rather than through either habit or custom, is seen in the creativity of the participants in a deliberation. Participants will be more receptive to suggested solutions that involve a great deal of thought on the particular problem. Proposals that are justified with reasons such as "because that's the way we've always done it" or "because the school across town is doing it" will be heavily critiqued because the words of the speaker show that he or she does not recognize the uniqueness of the problem under consideration. Every problem is set in a context that is particular to that classroom or school.

A unique problem requires a creative solution. An insightful solution may be proposed by one person or it may be a combination of many ideas. Weaving ideas together can be tricky because sometimes combining powerful thoughts can dilute them, but, on the other hand, sometimes combining complementary ideas can lead to a potential solution. This does not imply that the solution an individual or group chooses must be a compromise of the various perspectives; some perspectives are incompatible and cannot be combined. So although the chosen course of action may not have unanimous support from all perspectives, everyone should agree that the proposed solution has the best interest of students' or others in mind.

Deliberative inquiry is a continuing process. Solving a problem involves looking at it from various points of view and then reflecting deeply on how these perspectives connect, or do not connect, with our own views. But just when you think you have found a course of action to solve the problem, you may realize that it does not fully address the problem, the problem has changed or a new problem emerges. In other words, deliberating and playing with ideas never stops and you may have to go back to the beginning. If it did, then personal growth would stop. The puzzle is always in progress and open to new interpretations.

FOUR ELEMENTS OF DELIBERATIVE INQUIRY

Webster's definition of deliberation provides a nice overview of the term; however, we have seen that *deliberative inquiry,* when guided by teaching for democratic living, possesses four important characteristics: (1) creating a caring environment that minimizes fear and defensiveness, (2) exploring and defining problems from multiple points of view, (3) generating creative solutions through the consideration of differing perspectives, and (4) selecting and assessing the outcomes of a particular course of action.

Creating a Caring Environment

Fear can thwart the deliberative process. Palmer (1998) believes that one of our deepest fears is:

> The fear of having a live encounter with alien "otherness," whether the other is a student, a colleague, a subject, or a self-dissenting voice within. We fear encounters in which the other is free to be itself, to speak its own truth, to tell us what we may not wish to hear. We want those encounters on our own terms, so that we can control their outcomes, so that they will not threaten our view of the world and self. (p. 37)

Inquiring into other points of view may feel disconcerting because there is a chance that we may change the way we look at the problem and the way we view ourselves. If a viewpoint alters our own, we may incorrectly assume that the other viewpoint is right and ours is wrong. A perspective cannot be "wrong" if it is generous and generative to the problem-solving process. No perspective should be denied the opportunity to be expressed because others fear its impact. We can recognize whether or not fear is in our minds by being aware of our own thoughts:

> Attention to self-talk during fear states reveals that a person's thinking generally runs along the lines of, "What about me? What if I don't get my way? What if I don't get my share? I may be inconvenienced. Are they better than me? What's wrong with me? Why won't they listen to me? What if I fail? Will I be hurt? Will I be alone?" The focus is on oneself, not on others, and on getting, not giving. (Agnes, 1999, p. 173)

If these questions pop into our heads during a deliberation, then we are no longer caring about others and we have stopped any potential growth as teachers. Deliberations must occur in an environment where participants do not exhibit self-doubt and feel intimidated.

Individual deliberations will be productive if you are confident in your ideas and embrace challenges to these ideas by looking at multiple perspectives. Do not avoid clashes between perspectives; the confrontation may illuminate nuances in your ideas that could not be seen before. Periodically check whether you are deliberating with your best caring self by asking yourself the following questions: Am I putting the interests of others, such as my students, ahead of my own interests? Am I running away from particular perspectives? Am I thinking about the problem in the same way as when I started deliberating and playing with ideas two days ago? Your thoughts on the problem will change if you are honestly looking at the problem from different angles in order to understand the big picture.

Group deliberations require an additional element of trust among participants for discussions to thrive. Trust is not built in an environment where participants fear each other's views. However, participants should not "play nice" and accept alternative perspectives without any questions. Deliberating needs to take place in an environment where everyone feels free to exchange and critique ideas in a way that validates those ideas. To monitor the environment, group members should ask themselves the following types of questions: Did I ask him what past experiences influenced his interpretation of the problem? Did I tell her that I agree with her potential solution to the problem and give reasons that support hers? Why did he stop talking when we started to weigh the consequences to possible solutions and how can I draw him back into the discussion? Caring individuals who have confidence and build trust can minimize personal fears.

Examining and Describing the Problem

The first task in a deliberation is to define the problem. We often put the cart before the horse by brainstorming solutions to the problem before clearly articulating what the problem is. A description of the problem is vital so that the deliberative process can move forward productively within certain boundaries. Roby (1985) suggests that individuals identify specific details in a problematic situation, formulate these meaningful details into discrete problems, and weigh and choose among problem formulations.

We can raise a number of questions to clarify the problem situation. What does this problem encompass? Can the problem be broken down into smaller problems? How do I/we decide which description of the problem is best? Can the various perspectives on the problem be integrated in some way? How many perspectives should be considered before we feel that our description of the problem is exhaustive? Through the course of posing questions like these, the problem will be continually redefined until a consensus is reached.

Generating Creative Solutions

Listing possible solutions to the problem requires deep reflection on what is in the best interests of everyone involved, especially those who are affected by the action such as students. Individuals should formulate solutions to the problem, rehearse consequences of the solutions, and weigh and choose the solution (Roby, 1985). To select one solution out of many possibilities, we can ask a number of questions. Which perspective does a particular solution reflect? Do some of the solutions share some common characteristics? What consequences for a given solution can I (we) not accept? How do I (we) choose which solution to the problem is best? The more creative the questions are, the more creative the proposed solutions will be.

During the process of rehearsing consequences of the solutions, individuals may need to revisit questions that define the problem. A given solution may only partially address the problem, implying that more than one possible solution must be employed. In addition, while deliberating on various solutions, the discussion may point to a weak or inappropriate definition of the problem. Alternating between thoughts on describing versus solving the problem while always checking for a caring environment illustrates the nonlinear nature of deliberation. The discussion does not proceed in one direction; it is a playful exercise that goes off in whichever direction is applicable at that moment in time. No one can predict the course a deliberation will run.

Selecting and Assessing a Course of Action

Once a solution is decided upon and action is taken, individuals need to assess whether or not the course of action solves the problem. We can raise a number of questions. Did the action address the entire problem? What were the outcomes: good, bad, anticipated, unanticipated? How should these outcomes be assessed? Who does the assessing? Did the outcomes create another set of new problems? How does the school community perceive our course of action? Were there perspectives that need to be considered in the next round of deliberations?

In theory, deliberative inquiry is a continuous trial-and-error process. Reality prevents many deliberations from continuing indefinitely due to time and/or money constraints. But when you deliberate on ways to improve your teaching practice, this process is never ending simply because there will always be one more perspective to consider, one more solution to ponder, and one more action to take.

Looking at Figure 4.1 one last time, deliberative inquiry begins with a puzzle and ends with the creation of a unique picture. This picture is more than just the sum of its discrete parts. It is a holistic solution to a complex educational problem. Creating this solution may take longer when you are deliberating by yourself, but it can still be accomplished. Collaborating with others may expedite the problem-solving process, because sometimes others can see what we miss. Furthermore, when we collaborate with others, they may fit the pieces of the puzzle together in a way that would never occur to us. Although the picture is more than the sum of its parts, we should be conscious of each "piece" of our final solution. Because one "piece" in the wrong place can negatively impact the entire outcome, we should continually reflect on the problem-solving process as a whole. To integrate deliberative inquiry into our daily problem-solving efforts is a challenging professional standard; however, it is a tangible way to show that we care for our students and their lifelong growth. Deliberative inquiry is an essential component of teaching for democratic living.

INQUIRY SCAFFOLDING

The advice and questions that have been offered as guidance for *deliberative inquiry* can be synthesized into the following professional study scaffolding:

- Are my individual or group deliberations guided by a sense of generosity and generativity?

- Am I inquiring in a way that is sensitive to the perspectives of others? Could my deliberations be described as caring?

- In an effort to find creative solutions, am I considering diverse ways to define a problem?

- Am I being sufficiently imaginative in the solutions I am considering?

- Am I considering different ways to assess the consequences of my solutions?

Teacher Narrative*

Ohio's efforts to improve its schools are reflected in Senate Bill 55. This legislation requires school districts to adopt policies and procedures, beginning in the 1998–1999 school year, whereby they must assess each student's reading level at the end of the first, second, and third grades. Individual school districts must notify the parent or guardian of each student identified as reading below grade level and offer intervention services. The legislation also leads up to the "fourth-grade guarantee," which becomes effective in the 2000–2001 school year. This guarantee requires fourth graders to pass the reading component of the fourth-grade proficiency test before they can go on to the fifth grade.

As a third-grade teacher, I was particularly interested in how my school district would identify students who needed extra help in

---

*Contributed by Patricia Armstrong.

reading and implement these reading intervention services. Would my students finally get the help that they needed or were these tests just more hoops for my students and I to jump through? This legislation inspired me to get involved. In the summer of 1998, I was part of a district pilot program that was an experimental and proactive approach to providing help to those students completing first through third grades. Since some of the educators in my school district disputed the expectations set forth by Senate Bill 55, a committee was formed to discuss the establishment of reading standards and assessments. As a member of this committee, I witnessed how the interchange of philosophies and attitudes impacted the creation of new policies unique to my school district. Looking back on this experience, I see that our deliberations were more than a bunch of meetings to go to; they made us think about our purpose as teachers and how to best address the needs of our own students. Opening my mind to new ideas and perspectives is an important tool that I can take with me to my classroom.

I will maintain that reading is the core of all education. Within this philosophical framework, I contend that students have the right to be actively involved in their education. Each child should be educated in a way that best fits his or her own needs. Therefore, it is my responsibility, as an instructional leader, to provide the best learning experience possible for each child. Good teaching takes place if it is based on a solid foundation of community learners and leaders who emphasize the importance of student achievement and professional growth. Only then can this foundation reflect the vision needed for school improvement (Fawcett and Gaski, 1998).

While reading many articles to stimulate my inquiry into education, I continuously reflect back on my philosophy and how it fits with the most current and available research for the students in my classroom. For example, in an article entitled, "Catch Them before They Fall: Identification and Assessment to Prevent Reading Failure in Young Children," Torgeson (1998) supports the idea that children who get off to a poor start in reading rarely catch up. This crucial curriculum consideration is why I am interested in being involved in the changes in my district. I feel I can touch so many students when I get involved in decisions that are part of a solid foundation for our district's educational services.

Senate Bill 55 was created by Ohio legislators who believed that students should achieve a minimum level of competency in various subjects, such as reading. They took notice of the many children reading below grade level and decided that the way to solve this problem was to have teachers administer statewide proficiency tests to decide who is behind in their reading skills. Every day I work with students who are not reading at the same level as their classmates, but how do I determine whether or not they are reading "at grade level"? Are the Ohio proficiency tests a good measure of a student's reading ability? Is a student's poor performance in reading just a symptom of a larger problem? The legislators assumed that the problem—students reading below grade level—was straightforward. Instead, this problem opens the door to many questions, including "What does it mean to read 'at grade level'?" How our committee designs student assessments that lead to intervention depends on how we view this problem.

The goal of our first meeting was to begin to develop the policies and procedures that would be used to determine if a student is reading at grade level. Our ideas were based on the literature that describes what students should be able to do at different points in time. This information was very helpful, but we felt that knowing our colleagues' experiences with their students would be equally valuable. So we left the meeting on the hunt for information that would support or poke holes in our newly created standards. We talked and shared some of the established language arts beliefs informally with our specific grade-level teams and with staff members in our own schools. I got various reactions from my colleagues that I work with every day. They made excellent points that I had not even thought of! I still feel strongly about my particular beliefs in language arts, but they just gave me a wide-angle lens to look through. It made me wonder, how do teachers come to their beliefs about teaching reading? Can these beliefs change? How do they change? They will need to change if we implement new standards that contradict their stance. Will my beliefs change? In what ways do my beliefs impact my students?

When the committee reconvened to share what we had found out, I felt very comfortable sharing my beliefs and the beliefs of the staff at my school. This information would be useful in revising our first draft of the standards, which we needed to hammer out. We also developed the diagnostic assessment tools at each grade level, which will be used to determine if a student is reading at grade level. We spent time comparing reading programs at the Warren City schools and the Upper Arlington City schools. Their creative ideas spurred us to lively discussions about the craft of reading instruction, but we always kept in mind how our students, staff, and community are different from their counterparts in these school districts. These programs just provide a launching point for new ideas!

At this time, I was delighted to have been selected to meet with our assistant superintendent independently in order to share my thoughts and feedback of our progress thus far. This lengthy meeting was an opportunity for us to understand what this change might look like in the district's elementary classrooms. I felt that I could talk openly with her about the possible consequences of new standards and assessments. How would they affect my day-to-day teaching? Would I have more or less "say" about what goes on in my classroom? How do I decide whether the new standards and assessments meet the needs of my students? Can a teacher disagree with the standards and/or assessments and make his or her own judgments in certain cases? How will parents feel about the instruction based on these standards in my classroom? Not only did I feel my strong philosophical beliefs about making changes in the language arts area were respected, I maintain it was part of my professional responsibility to help lead these modifications in the learning environment in my classroom and in the entire community. We knew, and still know, that this process will need constant revision.

At another meeting, we divided into two groups to accomplish specific tasks. One group was charged with the task of developing formative student evaluations that could provide useful data during the course of the school year to support the results of the Riverside Off-Grade Proficiency and/or the Ohio Fourth Grade Proficiency exam. These remodeled and newly developed assessment tools will need to have a consensus vote on the content and format. Another group aligned and established the reading standards for each grade level. The standards were edited to make them parallel between grade levels, as well. This was a challenging day, yet necessary in putting final philosophical differences on the table for "exit standards" discussions. I wondered whether it was possible to reconcile these differences. At what point do philosophical differences become a bad thing? Can I "step into their shoes" and truly understand where they're coming from? What would my teaching be like if I approached it from these other perspectives? It will be critical to continue to communicate with grade-level teams across the entire district again throughout the spring, during the summer literacy program, and over the course of our implementation years for genuine change to occur. This process of ongoing communication and reflection will affect why and how all teachers will implement the standards and assessments. This was and is **key!**

Throughout this process, the entire committee has been able to read several other articles to help us with our changing philosophies about reading instruction. One article was entitled "Just Read" (Wolf, 1998). This article outlined action research projects showing that, with parental support and school commitment, students can greatly increase the number of books that they read independently and raise their reading achievement levels. Another article, entitled "Effective Teaching and Literacy Learning: A Look Inside Primary Classrooms" (Cantrell, 1999), described the everyday literacy instruction of four teachers who successfully implemented reform practices. The adoption of these meaning-centered teaching practices did not result in an abandonment of specific skills instruction. On the contrary, the teachers highlighted in this study continued to provide skills instruction in meaningful contexts according to their students' needs. They frequently provided explicit skills instruction and grouped students as needed for reading and writing instruction. Through a balanced approach to literacy instruction that focused on the needs of their students, these effective teachers provided the foundation for higher literacy learning. Continuously reading articles like these has provided me with leadership opportunities to open up a conversation with other colleagues during this change in the language arts curriculum.

In order to determine if a student is reading at grade level, we needed to have a common set of expectations for our students. As leaders in the building grade-level meetings, we each began collecting the thoughts, recommendations, and beliefs on what the staff in our own schools perceived as evidence that our students are competent readers at their respective grade levels. Two considerations were foremost on my mind. First, I felt we needed to identify grade-level expectations for "competent" reading. We should be able to create a consensus around such outcome statements as "At the end of ___ grade, a competent reader can:___." Second, last year we used the Riverside Off-Grade Reading Test and/or district-developed CBE reading assessments to identify which students were reading below grade level. In order to be identified as a competent reader, the student was required to pass both of these measures. Are there other tools we should consider using? And how can our current grade-level competency based education (CBE) assessments be improved to help us make this decision?

At this point, teachers representing each grade level in each of the four elementary school buildings were assisted in establishing the standards and assessments that the school district will use to certify students as competent readers at their grade levels. In addition to the preceding questions, which were asked early on in the process, we have been able to informally and individually survey colleagues about their own beliefs regarding reading standards. Some of the questions asked have included:

1. What is Senate Bill 55, and what does it mean to you in your classroom?

2. How will Senate Bill 55 require adjustments in how you currently document and communicate student progress to parents?

3. What other changes do you feel have not been made, but need to be undertaken?

The responses to these questions fell into two camps. One group of teachers supported the legislation and understood the implementation process being undertaken. They maintained that this will "keep everyone honest and responsible" about the certification process. One teacher profoundly struck me when she said, "A course of study isn't something that can sit on a shelf anymore." She made it clear that some teachers continue to teach lessons not based on the curriculum, although I had difficulty understanding how this was possible. She felt that teachers will now be pushed to have the knowledge and skills to recommend a student for summer intervention and have the correct documentation to prove a student's need for intervention. She believed, and I agree, that this will be unsettling for many teachers. The teachers who oppose the legislation and the curriculum changes made comments such as, "Now that we have to test kids all the time, when will we teach?" They believe the state is controlling how and when we teach the different objectives in our classrooms. These responses are eye-opening to me because I believe that we really can't miss on the test when we teach the curriculum.

It will take a lot of time to reflect on our own and each other's perspectives before we come to a consensus on this particular issue. Although it was (and still is) a concern to me that this change will be long and slow, I have learned to work on being more patient with the process of change. I found that deliberation is not just a product of talking, but a process of questioning and pondering new ideas. The more questions that I ask about myself and others, the more I can inquire and find out more about myself as a teacher and the educational environment that I work in. Inquiring into these questions is frustrating because I know I can't find the answers to many of them. But these questions need to be asked in order for school improvement, including student achievement and professional growth, to occur.

REFERENCES

Agnes, K. J. (1999). Caring: The way of the master teacher. In R. P. Lipka & T. M. Brinthaupt (Eds.), *The role of the self in teacher development* (pp. 165–188). Albany, NY: State University of New York Press.

Cantrell, S. C. (1999). Effective teaching and literacy learning: A look inside primary classrooms. *Reading Teacher, 52* (4), 373–378.

Fawcett, G., & Gaski, M. (1998). Where do these things come from anyway? Making the Ohio proficiency test work for you, not against you. *Ohio Reading Teacher, 32* (3), 4–6.

Harris, I. B. (1986). Communicating the character of deliberation. *Journal of Curriculum Studies, 18* (2), 115–132.

McCutcheon, G. (1995). *Developing the curriculum: Solo and group deliberation.* White Plains, NY: Longman.

Neufeldt, V., & Guralnik, D. (Eds.). (1996). *Webster's new world college dictionary* (3rd ed.). New York: Macmillan.

Noddings, N. (1984). *Caring: A feminine approach to ethics and moral education.* Berkeley, CA: University of California Press.

Palmer, P. J. (1998). *The courage to teach: Exploring the inner landscape of a teacher's life.* San Francisco: Jossey-Bass.

Roby, T. W. (1985). Habits impeding deliberation. *Journal of Curriculum Studies, 17* (1), 17–35.

Schwab, J. J. (1978). In I. Westbury & N. D. Wilkof (Eds.), *Science, curriculum, and liberal education: Selected essays.* Chicago: University of Chicago Press.

Torgeson, J. K. (1998). Catch them before they fall: Identification and assessment to prevent reading failure in young children. *American Educator, 22* (1–2), 32–39.

Wolf, J. M. (1998). Just read. *Educational Leadership, 55* (8), 61–63.

CHAPTER 5

AUTOBIOGRAPHICAL INQUIRY

§

Sue Lyons was offered her first teaching position in a primary-grade building. Her family and friends, who had supported her during her years of undergraduate teacher preparation, enthusiastically celebrated this opportunity with her. Sue so wanted to become a great teacher. She loved learning and was determined to create the kind of first-grade classroom that would enkindle that same love in her students. She spent the summer months before school started as most new teachers do: constructing materials for her students to use, planning her first week of lessons, and hoping she would never lose the spirit and passion she felt at that moment.

Sue somehow knew that there was more to good teaching than being prepared with well-crafted lessons and being liked by her students. She seemed to be the kind of teacher who placed high value on her own professional growth and who would take risks, explore, and experiment to provide the most imaginative educational experiences for her students. Yet, Sue was young, she was inexperienced, and she was just beginning to understand that if she were to succeed at being a "good" teacher, she would have to be comfortable with who she was and what she was becoming—as a human being and then as a teacher. Recognizing Sue's need for guidance, her principal spent many hours with her, allaying her fears, calming some of her anxiety, supporting her enthusiasm, and encouraging her to ask herself right from the beginning: "What do I want my personal/professional life story to be?"

The principal knew that Sue Lyons would be facing many crossroads personally and professionally. She would be confronted with traditional, controlling approaches to teaching all around her. She would feel uncomfortable with fellow teachers eager to mold her into the types of teachers they were; and yet, she would want to get along with everyone and she would fear being alienated from the others. The principal realized that Sue was also afraid of losing that special excitement and joy that she had for teaching and learning and the compassion she felt for students. Most important, she realized that Sue's students' love for learning would be a direct reflection of her own personal fulfillment as a human being and as a teacher. That was when the principal decided to put Sue in touch with Linda Byers, a veteran first-grade teacher well respected for her courage, vitality, and sensitivity, who could not only help Sue survive the pressures of the first year of teaching, but could also challenge her with difficult questions and offer wise advice and friendship. Linda helped Sue balance her need to be liked and be part of the group with her need to develop as a teacher true to herself and her beliefs about children and schooling. Linda and Sue made time to struggle over the tough questions that helped them both grow as caring, reflective teachers: How can I understand who I am? Is my life story being written the way I want it to be? What kind of teacher am I becoming? How will my students remember me? Linda helped Sue realize that though there weren't any "correct" answers to these questions, they needed to keep asking them and to explore their responses on a deeper and deeper level in order to understand themselves better.

As that first school year progressed, Sue quickly learned that developing into the person and teacher who embraced democratic living in her life and in her classroom would not be an easy task. She found that thinking critically, creatively, and imaginatively about teaching and learning and treating children as responsible classroom citizens were not only uncommon practices among teachers at her school, but were threatening to them, as well. Many of the teachers with whom Sue worked expected her to comply with their notions of classroom management, pedagogy, and the teacher's role. They supplied her with reams of worksheets for the students' use, instructing her, "We all use these. They are organized by weeks of the school year and we all stay on the same schedule." They also coached her on how to ensure her first-graders' "success" on the standardized achievement tests given in October. They provided her with patterns the children were to use to produce cookie-cutter art projects. They shared with her their behavior management plans to help her with classroom "discipline."

Sue was confused and disappointed with these attitudes and teaching practices. They seemed to take all the joy out of her work with the children. Yet, Sue felt pressure from these teachers to conform to their ways of doing things. She and Linda spent a considerable amount of time reflecting on these situations, trying to identify the conflicts Sue was experiencing and exploring ways to resolve the problems. The problems did not disappear, but with Linda's help, Sue was able to be true to the beliefs about teaching and learning that were developing within her. She was able to respectfully decline the ideas and practices that were contrary to her beliefs and to create a classroom where independent and interdependent children shared responsibilities, were creative and imaginative, and found joy in their learning. And, as her children grew, Sue grew as well. Sue's early intuitive thoughts about teaching began to give way to strong convictions about her own identity and her role as a teacher. Sue knew she had begun the first chapter of her professional life story.

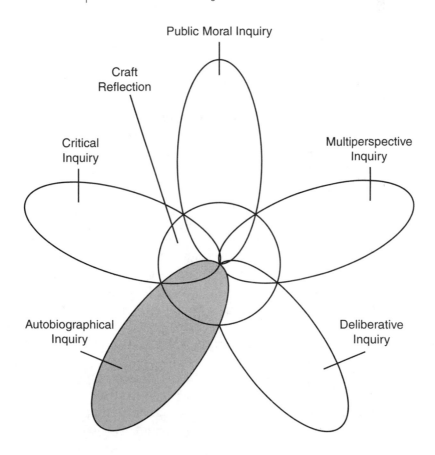

Through Linda Byers' invitation, Sue joined a group of parents and teachers from other schools who met regularly to explore their personal development through dialogue, study, and shared social experiences. They, too, were awakening to the principles of **democratic living** in and out of the classroom. They needed each other to offer support and challenge as they wrote their own personal stories. With them, Sue found kindred spirits with whom she questioned her practice, reflected on the difficult issues, and dialogued around problems in need of solution. Though Sue had a tacit understanding of what democratic living would mean for her and her students, engaging in critical self-discovery with her new professional friends helped her to reach a deeper level of self-awareness and to refine her philosophies of living and learning. Sue was developing into the kind of teacher she had hoped she would be, one who was filled with joy, passion, and wonder. And one whose students would remember as a loving, caring, yet challenging teacher.

INTRODUCTION

In recent months, our country has been shocked and saddened by horrible stories of children killing children in our schools. Probably every professional or armchair psychologist has attempted to understand this wave of violence. Issues of social violence, parental neglect, lack of self-discipline, the crumpled family structure, and the absence of God in the schools are just a few of the arguments that have surfaced to try to explain this sadness. Though different interest groups have voiced their preferred arguments, most of us can agree that somehow the needs of the human heart are not being satisfied in our schools today. Students and teachers cohabitate within "mega" schools sometimes composed of thousands of disconnected people. Teachers do not know their own colleagues, and students are disengaged and disenfranchised from adults and other students. Life in schools seems to be more about efficient use of time, space, and knowledge and less about nurturing individual spirits in need of love and understanding.

As current or future teachers, you share a responsibility with us to change those conditions. We believe that it is possible to bring human connectedness, caring, and compassion to a classroom. We believe that this must begin with each of us, as individuals, committed to a personal and professional life of self-exploration and inquiry. *We believe that through self-awareness you will awaken to who you are and what you believe in; and, in turn, your teaching will be steeped in discovery, inventiveness, and experimentation while grounded in deeply held beliefs and values.* We will use the term **autobiographical inquiry**, to describe this type of disciplined professional study.

The opening vignette introduced Sue Lyons as a first-year teacher embarking on a personal and professional journey of self-discovery. We hope it will offer you who are considering teaching as your profession guidelines for beginning to get to know yourselves better. The discussion that follows will encourage you to appreciate within yourselves the uniqueness that is *you* and to nurture the "call" to the teaching profession that your heart has heard. The suggestions offered here will help you become more attuned to another dimension of your professional self—a more *poetic* dimension that is cultivated and refined through personal soul-searching and continual revitalization. Through *autobiographical inquiry,* you challenge yourself to be in touch with the enchantment of teaching-learning transactions.

FIVE DIMENSIONS OF AUTOBIOGRAPHICAL INQUIRY

To become the responsible, caring, and inquiring adults we desire to be as teachers, we first need to challenge ourselves out of our comfort zones, and "develop the authority to teach, the capacity to stand [our] ground in the midst of the complex forces of both the classroom and [our] own [lives] . . ." (Palmer, 1998, p. 32). This requires an awakening of our authentic selves, a deepening of our capacity to think deeply and soulfully. It means developing a generous and generative spirit, a love for growth for ourselves and others, and a caring and compassionate nature. This necessitates our making some conscious choices, really planning the journey we are embarking on, knowing the direction we need to follow to *become* the person we want to be. And perhaps most important, it means making a *commitment* to the journey—no matter how long it takes, how difficult the terrain, or how stormy the weather along the way. As Palmer (1998) reminds us, "When I do not know myself, I cannot know who my students are. I will see them through a glass darkly, in the shadows of my unexamined life—and when I cannot see them clearly, I cannot teach them well" (p. 2).

Good teaching comes from the heart, from the true identity of the teacher, from a long and arduous journey of self-examination. It is *not* reliant on prescribed lesson packets, meticulously written lesson plans, efficient classroom management, and success on standardized tests. It *is* reliant on passionate teachers who are engaged in self-discovery and their own continuous growth; creative teachers excited about the possibilities of diverse thought; fair-minded teachers committed to the principles of equity; and caring teachers filled with a deep compassion for others. Good teaching is reflective of the teacher as person in a very holistic way. It is reflective of the mind, the heart, the soul, the very being that is the teacher. It is reflective of the teacher's place along the journey of "becoming." It is reflective of the teacher's disposition toward learning and the degree to which wonder, curiosity, and wisdom converge in his or her work.

This process of "becoming" is a lifelong endeavor. It is a process that will allow you to infuse your work with artistic expression of your love of teaching and learning. Five dimensions of *autobiographical inquiry* have been identified as a framework for getting to know yourself better for purposes of greater understanding, living, loving, and, ultimately, teaching. These dimensions are: (1) awakening to yourself, (2) traveling with a trusted guide, (3) associating with self-aware others, (4) engaging in dialogue, and (5) becoming the individual you desire to be.

Awakening to Yourself

Though developing a social philosophy of living and teaching is enriched through interaction with others, it depends on your taking time to spend some contemplative moments alone and asking yourself some deeply personal questions:

- Am I attending to the needs of my heart and soul?
- How can I begin to understand who I am, how I am, and why I am?
- What can I say I truly believe in?

It is often said that real growth occurs in the quiet times, the down times, the times uncluttered with the busyness of daily life. This means that you need to set aside time for regular meditation or prayer sometime during a hectic day. Some people rise early in the morning when the house is quiet to find time alone. Others find moments of peaceful meditation just before retiring. For you, finding that time may mean spending time in nature, enjoying a walk in the woods in the beauty of each passing season. It may mean losing yourself in the sun and sand on a beach and finding greater purpose in the majesty of the waves. It may mean fishing alone in a mountain stream where you are conscious only of your thoughts and an occasional bite on the hook. Others may find peace quietly listening to Mozart, reading books that encourage introspection, or enjoying an art exhibit, while some people explore who they are through writing in a daily journal. Whatever shape this prayer or meditation takes in your life, it always means spending time *alone* with yourself, getting to know the real you and thinking about the direction your life is taking. This time allows for soul-searching, deep analysis of questions playing on your mind and heart, or expressions of gratitude for a life going well. What you will learn during these times alone with yourself will help you to know how to navigate the twists and turns along the road that is your life. The critical reflection that can become part of these quiet times will influence the choices you make. The self-knowledge you gain will help you to develop a personal "social philosophy." It will affect how you make decisions and solve problems in your personal and professional life. It will help you choose the "others" you associate with, how you interact with them, and the professional you eventually become.

Traveling with a Trusted Guide

Just as a trek through an unfamiliar backwoods requires a guide who knows the terrain, developing a social philosophy that honors democratic living in and out of the classroom is not an easy road to follow and calls for a trusted companion. Though our country was founded on the principles of democracy, those principles are not commonly practiced in our schools. Resisting the pressures of tight management, bureaucratic controls, and the status quo takes not only courage, but also the support of others. Teachers who courageously venture out in the direction of democratic living find themselves in territory at times both foreign and frightening.

Just as Sue Lyons, in the chapter's opening vignette, found support and guidance with the veteran teacher, Linda Byers, you, too, may find it helpful to cultivate a relationship with a trusted friend or colleague. You will need to find someone who embodies those ideals that may have begun to gel within you as a result of the time spent alone in prayer or meditation. You might begin by looking close to home for your guide—a relative, a family friend, a teacher in your building, someone you have met through church or civic activities. This guide, who would not only support you in your development but also challenge your thinking, would be respected for his or her commitment to a passion—vocational and/or avocational—and a mind engaged in continuous improvement and inquiry. This person would be known for his or her own authenticity, grounded in his or her personal beliefs yet respectful of others' ideas and approaches. This individual would be a responsible risk taker, less concerned with the way things have been done and more concerned with collaboration for creativity and invention. Though often quietly going about their lives without attention or fanfare, these individuals are those able to see things that you may not, to offer perspectives that would be enlightening and instructive to you, and to help you "activate the single voice, the inner captain, the crier atop the minaret, the shaman with the bull-roarer [within yourself]" (Levoy, 1997, p. 298). Your guide should be able to help you explore these and other such questions:

- What do I want my life story to be?
- How can I grow into this life story?
- Who might help me along the way?
- Whom should I choose as my teacher?

Sue Lyons was comfortable exploring these types of questions with Linda Byers. Fortunately for both of them, they found time to work and grow together. They could be seen engaging in long discussions after the students had gone home at the end of the day. The second year they worked together, they requested common planning periods to build in time for reflection and dialogue during the school day. They participated in professional development sessions and worked on local and state committees together. They also volunteered at the local playhouse together. Within the context of daily life in the school, Sue was able to explore her beliefs about living and teaching with Linda. They discussed "sticky" situations when Sue's beliefs and values were in conflict, when other teachers tried to impose their ideas on her, and when administrative expectations were in direct opposition to her beliefs in a democratic way of teaching and learning. As the first of many trusted and respected guides Sue would choose over the course of her career, Linda helped Sue to awaken the truth within herself, she saw in Sue that which Sue did not yet see in herself. Linda made sure Sue did not abandon her dreams and helped her to expand her ideas into perspectives she had not yet realized. She helped Sue keep her curiosity, her energy, her excitement, and her passion alive!

Associating with Self-Aware Others

When we are very young, especially during adolescence, we are surrounded by many "friends." A recent radio commercial reflected this social and developmental phenomenon when a high school–aged speaker listed her "*very* best friends," a total of probably ten other girls! When we begin to "grow up," however, we tend to become more selective and find our "best friends" to be much fewer in number. We sort out for ourselves who we are, who we want to become, and who will make the journey with us. We can do this by asking ourselves several questions:

- ๑ Is the road I am on taking me in the direction I want to go?
- ๑ Do I need to cultivate different habits?
- ๑ Do I need to develop relationships with different types of people?
- ๑ Do I need to engage in activities that have deeper and more lasting meaning for me?
- ๑ Are my friends also my teachers?

When you are serious about self-examination for the purpose of understanding your beliefs and social philosophies, you will find that associating with certain selected others is not only personally fulfilling but growth enhancing. If these others share beliefs in living a democratic life, they will exhibit a generous spirit and respect toward others while they accept responsibility for their own personal growth and development.

In your communities and schools, there will be those who love what they have chosen as their life's work, who are in a continuous act of becoming, and who never cease to reflect, to question, and to learn. They will be a support for you as you become the kind of person you desire to be and as you do the kind of work you have chosen to do. Linda helped Sue to realize that there really were others in schools who shared her beliefs and values and who also were longing to associate with a group of like-minded others.

Teaching professionals coming together *in this way* has not been the norm. Planning a field trip, organizing a bake sale, deciding when to schedule special subjects or recess have traditionally been the subject for teachers' problem solving together. Living the democratic life in and out of the classroom, however, requires educators to come together around subjects of significance. It requires digging beneath the impersonal, the technical, and the superficial to create and sustain dialogue around our inner lives, around meaning and authenticity that must be central in teaching and learning, and around issues that are of deeper significance, such as those concerning equity, diversity, and community.

As teachers new to the profession, you will have to explore your surrounding landscape to find other individuals who might support your efforts yet challenge you to continue to develop, to clarify, and to refine your beliefs and values. They may be found participating in professional study groups, book clubs, Friday lunch groups, and action research teams. Your trusted guide may know where to find them. They may not be at your own school but may be found where you volunteer or worship. Wherever they are, they are those individuals who seem to work from the heart, who demonstrate a soulfulness, and who exhibit a real passion for life itself.

With new friends, you may begin to explore activities you have not regularly enjoyed in the past. While Friday nights out with friends and Saturday afternoon football games can be great fun, you might find a different kind of fulfillment in attending to your more spiritual side. Visiting a museum exhibit, taking in a play, enjoying a touring dance troupe, or listening to an orchestral performance are ways to feed your soul. Appreciating the arts will help you develop the sensitivities that bring richness to your life and will enable you to live life's joys and sorrows more deeply. Chances are that the new friends who would join you in such activities would also challenge you to reflect on your feelings and experiences and to expand your thinking. These new friends can become those teachers you will need along your journey.

Engaging in Dialogue

So far, you've read about getting in touch with yourself, traveling with a trusted guide, and growing in the company of self-aware others. The word *dialogue* has been used several times to describe the kind of contemplative activity that might transpire within yourself or with others. This might be a good time to distinguish dialogue from superficial conversation. Guided by a spirit of discovery and exploration, the purpose of dialogue is to learn about yourself and others, to gain knowledge, insight, and understanding, to heighten sensitivity, to understand inconsistencies, and to alter existing mental schemas (Burbules, 1993). Though dialogue is central to *multiperspective inquiry* as discussed in chapter 3, it is just as important in *autobiographical inquiry*. Through dialogue, you are able to question, to respond, and to redirect to bring about a change in yourself, to reconstruct your understanding, and to decide on and refine priorities.

Dialogue is serious and deep discussion entered into with confidentiality, commitment, reciprocity, respect, and concern. Dialogue can only be achieved in a safe place. It cannot exist in threatening, hostile environments. It can only exist when individuals are open minded, egalitarian, inclusive, caring, loving, and constructively evaluative (Fay, 1987).

Dialogue can take place quietly—through prayer and meditation, journal writing, self-talk, drawing, painting, and sculpture. Dialogue can also take dramatic or musical forms. Watch and listen to an accomplished pianist perform in concert. You may become aware of the "dialogue" going on between the musician and his or her music. Such a "dialogue" comes out of a deep emotional, intellectual, and spiritual commitment to personal, aesthetically rich expression. If such poetics are possible in music, aren't they also possible in education?

Dialogue can, of course, exist verbally in a problem-solving or decision-making session in which the emphasis is on discernment, discovery, exploration, debate, and deliberation—perhaps in a session with other teachers deliberating over proposed curriculum changes, or with friends debating the social value of the new play you just saw together. This use of dialogue was the topic of chapter 4. Wherever or however dialogue takes place, it needs to be conducted with a loving heart and genuine caring. Dialogue is never easy; it can be exhausting. It tends to push and pull you to places you may not want to go. It takes courage and honesty, whether engaged in it by yourself or with others. Yet, its rewards are great; it helps us come to a wholeness of intellect, emotion, and spirit. It helps us to explore what is happening inside of us as we grow as individual persons and teachers (Palmer, 1998). And it strengthens us to be able to withstand the pressures that come from trying to live a life of democratic principles in an environment where they are not the norm. For these reasons, it is an invaluable tool as you discover who you are and what you want your life story to be.

Becoming the Individual You Desire to Be

However your journey of self-awareness begins—with your own contemplations, through the promptings of a trusted guide, or after reading this book—it will lead you to a "different way of regarding daily life and the quest for happiness" (Moore, 1992, p. 3). It will set you on the journey of defining what your life will be and what you will consider happiness. It will give your life depth and greater value and "enrich your identity" (Moore, 1992, p. 29). It will give you some idea of how to answer those very difficult questions posed earlier in this chapter:

How can I understand who I am? What do I desire to be? What do I want my life story to be? Is my route taking me to my desired destination?

Levoy (1997) writes about engaging in a "pow-wow" with your own soul (p. 133). What better way to dialogue with yourself! This form of self-exploration needs to be an ongoing conversation with yourself during which your intelligence, intuition, fears, joys, and challenges are called into question, explored, and understood maybe just a bit better. As Palmer (1998) suggests, self-awareness forces you to face your fears: fears of diversity—that there may not be one right answer, one viewpoint, one way, one experience; fears of conflict—that you may not have lots of "friends" around you, that your beliefs may unsettle or even anger others, that your values be may in direct opposition to those of the norm; fears of a possible loss of identity—that you might be risking losing your sense of self when confronted with conflicting ideas; and fears of having to change your life—that transformation, new values, and new ways of living may be called for.

Though sometimes fearful, self-awareness can, nonetheless, take you closer to knowing, understanding, living, and loving. As it supports you on your journey toward democratic living, it releases you from the need for control, for having all the answers, for perfection, and for criticism of difference. It helps you to embrace the "otherness of the world and to see more clearly which actions are life giving [for democratic living] and which are not," and, most important, "to participate more fully in your own destinies and the destiny of the world" (Palmer, 1998, p. 56).

Because you have been "called" to the noble profession of teaching, you have a responsibility to your students to nurture what Armstrong (1998) refers to as the "genius" within yourself. For without those poetic qualities of teaching—joy, sensitivity, curiosity, playfulness, imagination, creativity, wonder, wisdom, inventiveness, vitality, and flexibility—teaching is as he suggests "like soda pop without the fizzle" (p. 15). By traveling this road of self-exploration, you will awaken the poetry within you. You will begin to construct your identity and your life story around your noblest aspirations. As noted earlier, if you choose this journey, it will not be an easy road to follow. You will be personally challenged to heed the advice of the poet,

Rilke: "Be patient toward all that is unsolved in your heart and try to love the questions themselves. . . . Live the questions now. Perhaps you will then gradually, without noting it, live along some distant day into the answer" (Palmer, 1998, p. 86).

INQUIRY SCAFFOLDING

Throughout this chapter, advice and questions have been offered as guidance for *autobiographical inquiry*. This material can be synthesized into the following professional study scaffolding:

- Do I daily attend to the poetics of teaching and learning?
- Can I articulate my deepest professional beliefs?
- Do I consciously cultivate the noblest possibilities of growth for both my students and myself?
- Do I seek opportunities to establish trusting collegial relations?
- Do I associate with people who are consciously engaged in their own journey of self-awareness?
- Whenever possible, do I engage in open-hearted dialogue with others?
- Am I open to the questions that touch on my purposes for living and for being "called" to the teaching profession?

Teacher Narrative*

Reflection has been at the heart of my efforts toward good teaching as well as the key to my own spiritual growth. Knowing who I am and what I believe in has allowed me to teach from the heart. "What do I believe?" a question I ask myself over and over again, is always followed by "How do my actions in the classroom reflect those beliefs?" Being in touch with my spiritual side puts passion into the things that I do. I believe that I have been called to be a teacher and

---

*Contributed by Tebra Stepnicka.

I was meant to work with children through education. When I reflect on the responsibility I have accepted to help each student learn to his or her greatest potential, I am often overwhelmed! But I find reassurance because my faith has provided me the support I need to meet this challenge.

As each school year begins, I pray over my class list, knowing that without spiritual guidance I cannot succeed at the task set before me. I truly believe that each student is placed in my classroom for a reason, so I pray that I'll be sensitive to each child's needs. At times, the intense responsibility I feel for helping each child lies heavy on my heart and can become all consuming. As I drive home each evening, I think about my day, my words, and my actions, and I evaluate myself on how effectively I have met my students' needs. Some days I feel euphoric, other days I feel disappointed. I often lament how routines of the day or my attitude caused me to miss a very important learning moment. Sometimes I have to accept what I consider my own inadequate performance. This, however, spurs me on to become more attuned, more attentive, and more responsive the next day, hopefully learning from my experiences.

The questions I ask myself about the culture of my classroom have been more insightful to me than the questions I have asked about how I deliver a lesson. Do I believe all children can learn? Do I treat boys differently from girls? I recognize that I have a soft spot in my heart for boys who walk that fine line between being mischievous and disrespectful. Do those who do not fit this description feel less valued? Do my students, especially the girls, see that bend in me? Do I treat children with disabilities differently? Am I more sensitive to affectionate children than those with a chip on their shoulders? Do I treat my students equally or fairly—very different approaches? I struggle with these questions daily as I interact with my entire class. I so want each child to know that he or she has been hand chosen by a greater being to be in my class. Yet, how do I deal with my feelings of frustration and panic when I don't seem to be making progress? I turn to my prayer life and my devotional time as a source of inspiration and support. As I read or listen to music, I often record the thoughts and words I am challenged with. One of my favorite songs is about the different ways God can lay His calming spirit upon me—how He has the power to calm the stormy waters around me, but not always; while other times He makes His presence known to me, His child, and calms my "stormy" emotions. I gain strength knowing that sometimes the situation with struggling will somehow take care of itself. If it doesn't, it that often becomes calmed in the midst of the challenge. I even realize a new plan.

What I believe and don't believe about democracy in our and our schools is something I only recently have begun to art I struggle with the pure meaning of democracy applied to issu situations in conflict with my own beliefs. Recently, a nearby cit ernment granted a permit to the Ku Klux Klan to demonstrate busy Saturday afternoon in front of the Justice Center. That group has the right to distribute their hate propaganda doesn't well with my soul. Because their views are so hurtful to so many, th right to exercise free speech does not resonate well with me. Yet, worry. How do I talk about such issues without biasing my student toward my thinking? I wonder about my internal biases. I often reflect on how my own feelings and actions affect the students in my class. Are my preconceived notions getting in the way of my teaching? Are my biases a help or a hindrance to my teaching? How has my experience, education, and life colored my views and, as a result, my teaching? I struggle to understand viewpoints I don't hold. Being a reflective professional has forced me to deal with these issues and to be willing to make necessary changes in my thinking and teaching.

Knowing my beliefs is only the first step. The next crucial step is asking myself continually how my actions reflect my beliefs. I honestly have not figured this out as yet. But I do know that in order to examine my actions objectively, I need help. At first, I had a hard time identifying a kindred spirit. Working in a public school made it somewhat difficult to openly discuss my faith walk. Moreover, I was new to my building and I didn't really know the climate. Nancy, a special education teacher, and I began to collaborate daily about the students that we shared in my class. A true pioneer of inclusion of special-needs children in the regular education classroom, Nancy was looking for a teacher to team with her. She asked me to become that teacher. In that way, we began a wonderful journey together, exploring and challenging each other personally, professionally, and spiritually. The more we worked together, the more we discovered that our philosophies about education resounded within each other's souls. Nancy and I planned together, taught together, and assessed together. She and I lovingly held each other accountable to our beliefs and values. At one point, I became worried about special treatment that I had given to a child with special needs. Nancy and I were able to dialogue around questions to help me reflect on the situation. Had I adequately modified his assignment? Should he have been able to complete the assignment in a timely fashion? Was I treating him more fairly because of his disability?

Working with Nancy, I discovered many wonderful insights about my teaching. We even took our show on the road and shared with other teachers the joys of collaborative teaching. Not only did we share in the successes of our teaching, but we also consoled and supported each other through disappointments and failures. We found that it takes time, patience, and courage to find and open up to a trusted friend. Thinking about those days before we worked together, I wonder how I was able to survive the isolation. I have grown tremendously through our relationship.

We continue to encourage as well as challenge each other. We stick together and support each other, especially when our beliefs come into conflict with those of our colleagues. A situation concerning interdisciplinary teaching became such an issue for us. I believe that for many reasons thematic, interdisciplinary teaching is best for students. Though it involves many hours of planning to integrate different areas of the curriculum, the rewards of students' understanding are well worth it. My colleagues at my grade level are not as passionate about thematic teaching as I am. The team wanted to departmentalize science instruction. They felt it would be more efficient if teachers planned and became an expert on one topic rather than on six. I worried about how this could benefit children. Was this a better way of teaching science or simply a way to reduce teacher planning time? As Nancy and I dialogued with each other, the fact that this idea did not fit with my beliefs about children and learning became evident. My response to the team's initiative had negative results for me. My colleagues' reactions both hurt me and made me defensive. How could they ostracize me in this way? I was labeled as "too dedicated," a negative rather than a positive in their eyes. They accused me of not being a "team player." It was only by being in touch with who I am as a teacher and with what I believe is good teaching and having Nancy as a support that I was able to make a difficult decision like this, dissent from the norm, and live with the consequences. The time we have spent together has helped to fortify and strengthen my understanding of who I am and what I believe. My teaching years with Nancy have been my best.

As I continue to grow professionally, I wonder about the direction I am taking. A few years ago, I was encouraged by colleagues to pursue a leadership role in education. Though that seed had been planted early on in my teaching career, my continuing my education and raising a family of four children were in conflict. Because of changes in my personal life, I finally have been able to return to graduate school. There I have found the group of "select others" my soul had been seeking! I was introduced to the ideas of a feminine way of knowing and leading, which resounded so clearly within me. I found I shared many of my feelings and experiences with other women. The affirmation I sought, without really understanding it, was discovered through the guidance of a very special professor. She shared a book by Mary Catherine Bateson with us. Here I found the words I had been searching for:

> Unless teachers can hold up a model of lifelong learning and adaptation, graduates are likely to find themselves trapped in obsolescence as the world changes around them. Of any stopping place in life, it is good to ask whether it will be a good place from which to go on as well as a good place to remain. (Bateson, 1990, p. 14)

As I unveiled new ideas through reading and discussion in her classes, I found opportunities to discuss my new-found knowledge with our school district's assistant superintendent, a woman who has become such an inspiration and friend. Dialoguing with her and forming my own beliefs about the field of educational administration and the professional field of teaching has been a fulfilling experience personally, as well as professionally. Realizing the vision and the patience this woman has exhibited toward us, her colleagues, as we slowly "get on board" has been a real revelation to me. Her willingness to discuss new ideas, to encourage my leadership qualities, and to challenge my thinking has been a blessing. Through my relationship with her, and those with my graduate school peers and professors, I am finding real exhilaration! I know from discussions with my peers that this is not the norm. I have found two women in leadership positions willing to guide me and encourage me. I see this phenomenon as another way that God has blessed my life. My faith in His journey for me has placed me in the right places at the right times. I have been encouraged and enabled to reach out. I have made connections that are beneficial to my growth, as well as to the growth of those with whom I share relationships. Teaching is so much more than delivering lessons; it is an opportunity to challenge my students to become critical thinkers, inquiring minds, and lifelong learners. By experiencing such growth myself, I am better able to model this life for them and to live a personal axiom that I learned a long time ago: "To teach is to touch a life forever."

REFERENCES

Armstrong, T. (1998). *Awakening genius in the classroom*. Alexandria, VA: Association for Supervision and Curriculum Development.

Bateson, M. C. (1990). *Composing a life*. New York: Plume Books.

Burbules, N. C. (1993). *Dialogue in teaching: Theory and practice*. New York: Teachers College Press.

Fay, B. (1987). *Critical social science: Liberation and its limits*. Ithaca, NY: Cornell University Press.

Levoy, G. (1997). *Callings: Finding and following an authentic life*. New York: Three Rivers Press.

Moore, T. (1992). *Care of the soul*. New York: HarperCollins.

Palmer, P. J. (1998). *The courage to teach*. San Francisco: Jossey-Bass.

CHAPTER 6

CRITICAL INQUIRY

Nancy Jefferson is a young teacher at an urban elementary school with a racially and economically diverse student body. Although most students are from white middle-income homes, a realignment of district boundaries the year before her arrival and an upscale urban-renewal development meant an increase in both lower income students of color and wealthy white families. Nancy has had offers to go elsewhere, but she believes her energy and talents would be best used in this district. She believes that all of her students can learn, that their cultural identities should be affirmed, and that one of the best ways to understand students' backgrounds is to get involved in community activities.

Nancy learned during her student teaching experience to include literature and other activities that build on her students' cultural backgrounds. She understands the importance of culturally responsive teaching; but during her first year, she was surprised by the lack of multicultural literature in her required third-grade curriculum. Now in her second year, with her head above water, she decided she would like to augment the curriculum. When she asked her department head about the existing book list, she was told that the new school board believed that teaching the classics was the best way to increase test scores. When she asked around in the teachers' lounge about some recommendations for culturally relevant books, she was either answered with blank stares or told simply, "Don't rock the boat." But privately, Nancy felt uneasy that so many of her students' cultural backgrounds seemed to be ignored. It just does not sit right with my responsibilities to my students, she thought.

A fellow worker at a local community center, where Nancy served as a volunteer tutor a few hours a week, recommended a book her daughter was reading. It was about a young African American girl and her struggle with having different hair and skin than the other students in her class. This book had won many awards in children's literary circles, and Nancy believed the students would love it. She photocopied pages from the book for students to take home so they could act out part of the story. A few days later, the principal, who had been informed about Nancy's use of the book, came into class and asked Nancy to come to an after-school meeting for a discussion of her third-grade curriculum. She went in smiling, expecting to be greeted by people she had met in the school and community. Instead, she was confronted by several angry parents. One called her a racist and said she was mocking them. Another challenged the wisdom of her curriculum decisions.

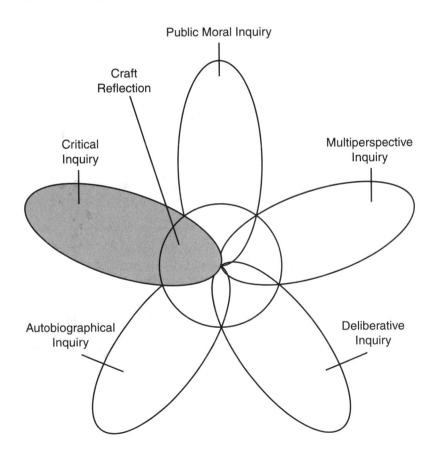

When Nancy went to school the next day, she discovered that several parents had kept their children home. Some teachers weren't speaking to her, and a few others just said, "We told you so." By the end of the day, Nancy knew that she was in for the challenge of her young professional life, but she felt ready and determined. Because many of her students and their parents, as well as the principal and a number of her colleagues, supported her culturally responsive efforts, she felt she could persist. Though there might be local political pressures to avoid the use of certain culturally relevant material, she felt that, ethically speaking, she had no other choice. She certainly had much to learn, but she would not be deterred.*

INTRODUCTION

This chapter's opening vignette sends a clear message. To challenge the status quo requires courage and conviction. Nancy Jefferson chose to go beyond the prescribed curriculum because she felt the need to affirm the cultural experiences of her students. She questioned the effectiveness of current teaching methods, and she took time to learn about the community. Because she was a new teacher, Nancy did not understand the depth of the racial tensions in her school district. Though she remained committed to her professional convictions, the vignette ends with her need to sharpen her critical inquiry capacities, which is the focus of this chapter.

Critical inquiry addresses the social, economic, and political relations among people. When critical inquiry is integrated into teaching, it is often called *praxis*. Lather (1991) describes *praxis* as educational practice that is explicitly committed to critiquing the status quo and building a more just society. Through critical inquiry, we confront social and personal inequities; and by taking on such challenges, we breathe ethical meaning into

---

*We wish to thank Melanie Hameed, a high school English teacher in Warren, Ohio, for her many insights into critically informed teaching. Her ideas and her passions contributed to this opening vignette and to the organization of this chapter.

our instruction. As critically informed teachers, we refine and enact our passion for justice and fair play.

THREE COMPONENTS OF CRITICAL INQUIRY

Critical inquiry possesses three important, overlapping components: (1) visionary pragmatism, (2) political awareness, and (3) ethical responsibility. We now turn our attention to each of these important considerations.

Visionary Pragmatism

Sirotnik (1991) writes: "Critical inquiry begins with the answer 'No!' and continues with a process of informed reflection and action guided by explicit, normative considerations" (p. 245). When we are critical, we don't believe everything we are told, and we don't just rely on pleasing appearances. We ask penetrating, unsettling questions, and we think in a deeply visionary way about the possible consequences of our actions. Cherryholmes (1999) describes this critical attitude as the pragmatic approach to educational practice:

> Pragmatism looks to consequences that we endlessly bump up against. We respond to and live with outcomes all day, everyday. These results come from our actions and those of others. They also come from events beyond our control. Pragmatists anticipate outcomes. They look to imagined and actual outcomes . . . . Pragmatists conceptualize the world where we, all of us, are constantly thrown forward as the present approaches but never quite reaches the future. Pragmatism is a discourse that attempts to bridge where we are with where we might end up. The future, the other unknown side of this bridge, can certainly be forbidding. There is little, if anything, that we can say with confidence about it. The temptation is to look backward. Pragmatism resists this siren's song by accepting the challenge to look ahead. (p. 3)
>   . . . Tracing consequences can be thought of as the present looking forward. And the present itself is a construction of past experiments. A history of the present, therefore, is contextually important in imagining outcomes. As individuals, we are who we are because of our location in multiple arenas; some are

historical . . . and some are social and political. What we can conceive is simultaneously made available and constrained by such factors. (p. 109)

When we are pragmatic in Cherryholmes' visionary sense, we continually wonder if we are seeing things correctly. We pursue deeply penetrating questions because we want to get to "the truth of the matter." Due to our critical commitments, we are as willing to challenge our own beliefs and practices as those of others. We understand that there are no "sacred cows" in education and that whatever has been constructed can be questioned, modified, and even significantly altered.

Critical inquiry is closely linked to multiperspective inquiry, the topic of chapter 3, because "truth" for one person may not be "truth" for another. Take, for example, the case of a teacher asking why one particular child's parents do not come to conferences. Teacher A answers the question by assuming the parents are not interested in their child's education. Teacher B, perhaps having more knowledge of the family, assumes both parents probably had to work. Whose truth is correct? In this case, it depends on the contexts. Both answers could be true; but until we probe more deeply into the parents' situation, we do not know. Perhaps if we just dispensed with the idea that there has to be one answer to a problem, we can open ourselves up to a wide range of pragmatic considerations.

To cultivate your critical awareness as a teacher, you need to understand the social context of your students' learning. You need to know obvious things like how large the district is, how many schools, teachers, and students make up the district, but you also need to know the religious, racial, and ethnic makeup of the community. You need to find out if there are agencies and community organizations that can or do provide services to your students and their families such as Girl/Boy Scouts or Head Start. You need to know which businesses are the largest in the community. You need to know the history of your district. Has a levy failed recently? Has there ever been a teachers' strike? Are bussing policies in place? Have their been disputes, lawsuits, or firings? There are many, many questions to ask. Remember, teaching is not just about what is between the covers of the book and the walls of your classroom. In fact, to borrow a term from the business world, you must learn to think "outside of the box." You must think outside the four walls of your classroom.

Ladson-Billings (1994) talks about an experience that happened to her when she was in school. In a high school English class, she had achieved A's on all her work, but at the end of the quarter she found a C on her report card. When she asked the teacher for an explanation, she was told a C was the highest grade possible in the course. The course turned out to be a remedial English course, composed mostly of African Americans. In the end, she found that a computer error caused her placement in this class instead of the honors course she should have attended. But the teacher accepted the fact that anyone in the course should get no higher than a C regardless of his or her work. By ignoring this unfair practice, by not questioning it, this teacher was reproducing the unfairness that many nondominant group members experience in society as a whole.

Public schooling was created, in part, to help maintain society's freedoms (Greene, 1988), but freedom is a tricky subject with many subtle considerations. We may believe that all citizens in our country are endowed with freedom and that we live in an "equal opportunity" society. We may also believe that what is written in our country's Constitution provides all citizens with the power to overcome any obstacles standing in their way— what Greene (1988) calls an absence of interference. However, ask many members of subordinate groups, such as African Americans and Native Americans in the United States, if they view themselves as "free." Then think about society's deeply embedded structures. Do you think they're fair? Do you think all citizens have an equal opportunity to realize their potential? When you ask such questions, you are practicing critical inquiry.

Greene (1988) helps us understand that social imagination is an integral part of our critical work. She writes that educators must cultivate their "capacity to surpass the given and look at things as if they were otherwise" (p. 5). Teachers must envision how all citizens in their society could be liberated to live a deeply fulfilling life. She notes that both Thomas Jefferson and John Dewey believed that school was one place in society where this visionary work could occur, and she argues that teachers should help their students think deeply about the value of democratic living. Teaching "is an undertaking oriented to empowering persons to become different, to think critically and creatively, to pursue meanings, to make increasing sense of their actually lived worlds" (Greene, 1986, p. 72). As critical educators, we must help our students see both the overt and the covert obstacles in front of them, to understand these obstacles, and, ultimately, to see beyond them to a better life. These obstacles may be as commonplace as unfair tracking and grouping practices. We must be willing to challenge all of our instructional decisions, as well as all school district, local community, state, and national policies. We must constantly examine our surroundings in a constructive, visionary spirit. We must continually ask ourselves, "What are we doing now that could be done better?" In this progressive spirit, Shor (1993) stresses the importance of practicing a constructive social criticism: "But, the critical teacher who teaches for democracy and against inequality also has the right and the responsibility to put forward her or his ideas. The problem-posing teacher is not mute, value-free, or permissive" (p. 30).

Aronowitz and Giroux (1985) believe that teachers need to be "transformative intellectuals." These are people who, in the language of chapter 1, rely less on *habit* and *custom* and more on critical *intellect*. When teachers are transformative, they work for fundamental change. They openly embrace educational reform because they can envision a better society. More will be said about teachers as transformative leaders in the next and last chapter of this book.

Political Awareness

Paulo Freire, an influential Latin American theorist, describes the link between education and politics in his philosophy of schooling. He notes that all forms of schooling are political, even if teachers are not consciously aware of this aspect of their work (Freire, 1987). Decisions about curriculum, about teaching and who teaches, about standardized tests are all political. Critical teachers carefully think about manifestations of power in their classrooms, schools, and communities. Shor (1993) writes:

> Traditional education orients students to conform, to accept inequality and their places in the status quo, to follow authority. Freirean critical education invites students to question the system

they live in and the knowledge being offered them, to discuss what kind of future they want, including their right to reject authority and to remake the school and society they find. Education is politics because it is one place where individuals and society are constructed. Because human beings and their society are developed in one direction or another through education, the learning process cannot avoid being political. (p. 28)

Kincheloe (1999) points out the wide range of considerations associated with an awareness of power relations in education. He writes that critical inquiry "is especially concerned with how democracy is subverted, domination takes place, and human relations are shaped in schools, in other cultural sites of pedagogy, and in everyday life" (p. 71). He adds that critical consciousness helps an educator understand "how and why his or her political opinions, worker role, religious beliefs, gender role, and racial self image are shaped by dominant perspectives" (pp. 71–72). Working with Freire's ideas, Bartolome (1995) describes this far-reaching critical awareness as *political clarity:*

> Political clarity refers to the process by which individuals achieve a deepening awareness of the sociopolitical and economic realities that shape their lives and their capacity to recreate them. In addition, it refers to the process by which individuals come to better understand possible linkages between macro-level political economic and social variables and subordinate groups' academic performances at the micro-level classroom. It requires links between sociocultural structures and schooling. (p. 43)

Critically informed teachers understand that schooling is situated at the intersection of knowledge and power and that too often youth are socialized to become unquestioning, conforming members of an unfair society. They understand that, in general, social institutions such as schools reflect the values and beliefs of those who are economically, politically, and/or culturally dominant in society. Teachers with political clarity go to great efforts to ensure that, to the best of their ability, social injustices and inequities are not reproduced in their classrooms and schools. They want all students to receive equal opportunities for a life of continuing growth. They understand that they have an important "political" job that will affect their society's future. There is nothing neutral or value-free about what they do.

At this point, you may be wondering if you have the time and energy to develop your critical capacities. Life is stressful, after all, and teachers have a full plate. How can you be expected to practice critical inquiry reflection while immersed in the press of daily activities? Like many teachers, you may think, "My job is simply just to teach." If this is your position, ask yourself this question: *If teachers only work as subject matter specialists, how will students experience the joys and responsibilities of democratic living?* Shor (1993) notes the challenges of critically informed teaching:

> After long years in traditional schools, teachers become conditioned to lecture, to assert their authority, to transfer official information and skills, as the proper way for professionals to do their work. It is not easy for them to share decision-making in the classroom, to negotiate the curriculum, to pose problems based in student thought and language, to lead a dialogue where student expression has an impact on the course of study, and to learn with and from students. (p. 29)

Teaching for democratic living does involve many challenges, but the rewards outweigh the difficulties. When you teach in this way, you are helping your students with the quality of their lives. You have the deep satisfaction of knowing that you are providing your students with opportunities to live a thoughtful, personally meaningful, and socially responsible life.

Ethical Responsibility

An experienced teacher talks about his fourth-grade classroom. Though he speaks of overstuffed king-for-a-day chairs, bright art displays made of construction paper, and a store where good grades equaled cash, he touches on the core of his work when he says: "Nobody, but nobody messes with my kids. They understand that the classroom is their safe place and no one is going to take that from them." Do you know such teachers? They feel a deep need, a drive, and a desire to do the best they can for each of their students. Through their *autobiographical inquiry,* which was the topic of chapter 5, they recognize that something deep within them inspires their quest to lead the young into the wonderful world of learning. Because they have cultivated their self-awareness, they are deeply sensitive to their ethical responsibilities as educators in a pluralistic society with democratic ideals.

Hopefully, you are equally sensitive to the ethics of teaching. Hopefully also, you feel passionate about your chosen profession. Keep in mind that *compassion* is an important part of passion. Compassion is defined as "deep feeling for and understanding of misery and suffering and the . . . desire to promote its alleviation" (Gove, 1986). Compassion is composed of the prefix "com," meaning with, and the root "pati," meaning to suffer. Dedicated, caring teachers feel compassion for those they teach. They constantly worry about their students' educational well-being. They want to support their students' emergence as lifelong learners because they know that this approach to life is the best way to minimize human suffering.

The National Education Association (NEA) has a code of ethics for educators composed of two principles describing how teachers should relate to their students and their colleagues. The Preamble for this code of ethics begins as follows:

> The educator, believing in the worth and dignity of each human being, recognizes the supreme importance of the pursuit of truth, devotion to excellence, and the nurture of democratic principles. Essential to these goals is the protection of freedom to learn and to teach and the guarantee of equal opportunity for all. The educator accepts the responsibility to adhere to the highest ethical standards. (Strike and Soltis, 1985, p. xiii)

This understanding of professional ethics has guided the creation of this chapter and the book as a whole. Sirotnik (1990) highlights the ethical responsibility that lies at the heart of critical inquiry when he writes:

> To inquire is to be thoughtful, reflective, and informed: to seek and use information; to describe, explain, interpret and evaluate new and existing knowledge; and to be sensible be it quantitatively or qualitatively, inductively, deductively, or dialectically. To be critical is to question and question constructively; to appraise knowledge in the context of practice; to challenge existing knowledge and practice with an eye toward improvement; to situate knowledge and practice in historical, current and future perspectives . . . and to ethically

ground the actions that people take that affect the lives of others. (pp. 313–314)

As an ethically responsible teacher, you must move beyond "band-aid" solutions. You must seek out the source of the pain. The hurt may be due to social, political, or economic injustices touching on complex race, class, gender, disability, or sexual orientation issues; or it may be simply due to the fact that a student is the smallest person in the class. Your sense of ethics may require you to question an unfair curriculum practice, administrator, or school policy. It may require you to study the politics of your school district. Kanpol (1998) describes professional ethics as a covenant teachers build with their students—an often unspoken pledge to serve their best educational interests through the continuing critical examination of school and community practices. Teachers who work with an ethical covenant demand and create safe spaces for their students to flourish. They create a place where students can experience democratic living.

However, as the new teacher in the chapter's opening vignette learned, working as a critically informed educator can have its down side. Critical inquiry leads you into a challenging arena of complex and controversial educational issues. Debates have raged over the "cultural illiteracy" of today's students because they don't know Shakespeare but understand the relationship between poetry and rap. However, how should "cultural literacy" be interpreted in a pluralistic society with democratic ideals? Such a question is best answered through critical inquiry. The state of California has ended bilingual education, declaring that all students must speak English because it will benefit them in the long run. But is this the main reason for this change? Is the motivation really to save money? Is the purpose to force immigrants to drop their language-embedded cultural practices? Such questions are matters for critical inquiry.

Critically informed teachers focus on righting the wrongs of society. Such an enormous undertaking can feel overwhelming at times, so what is the best way to practice critical inquiry? Take one step at a time; carefully establish a supportive political base, maintain good working relationships, and, most important, turn your classroom into a place where students daily experience justice and fair play. Encourage your students to raise deep questions about the relationship between knowledge and power, help them understand that they can make the world a better place, and allow them to experience the joy of democratic living—at least for the hours they are in your classroom.

You have read in this book that teaching can be a professional practice that is informed by an *inquiry artistry*. You have learned that teaching can be much more than a skill-based, cookbook activity. However, cooking is a helpful metaphor to describe the process of critical inquiry. To cook, you must learn about the kitchen, how to measure the ingredients, and how to follow the recipe. But to become a master chef, you must also learn how to improvise, how to create, how to understand the chemical reactions taking place, how to mix the ingredients, and how to work with the strengths and weaknesses of your utensils and appliances. In becoming a master teacher, which is a career-long process, you must learn to inquire into and endeavor to understand what is going on in the lives of your students, in the school organization, in the local community, and in society as a whole. What is the nature of the power relations in each of these settings? When you ask such critical questions, you develop your capacities to teach for democratic living.

INQUIRY SCAFFOLDING

Throughout this chapter, advice and questions have been offered as guidance for *critical inquiry*. This material can be synthesized into the following professional study scaffolding:

§   How do you understand the social context of your students' learning? How does their life outside school impact their experiences within school?

§   Do you notice any injustices or inequities in the schooling process?

§   What is the nature of the power relations in your classroom, the school, the community, and the school district?

§   What vision of a just society guides your critical questions?

§   Based on the information you have gathered through your critical questions, what educational changes should be made?

§   Are your thoughts on educational reform based on a critical examination of contrasting points of view on the nature of the problem and how it should be solved? (Have you incorporated multiperspective and deliberative inquiries into your critical questioning?)

§   How can you constructively address the politics of this potential educational reform?

§   Assuming that you can act on your critical inquiries, what are the consequences of your reform activities? Have you made inroads into problems of injustice and inequity? Are students better able to experience democratic living? Do you feel you are properly practicing your professional ethics?

§   How can you engage in continuing cycles of critically informed problem solving? How can you make critical questioning an integral part of your professional learning?

Teacher Narrative*

Whenever I think about the role critical inquiry plays in my life and my teaching, I'm reminded of the sticker affixed to the bumper of my car. It reads, "If you're not outraged, you're not paying attention." Five years ago, as a first-year teacher, I ordered that single sticker from a catalogue that offered literally hundreds of witty choices. Each day as I walk to my car before driving to school, I read it for motivation.

It hasn't failed me yet.

Although it may sound like an oversimplified explanation, being critically mindful in life and in teaching is really a matter of paying attention—to power and its intersections with race, class, gender, sexual orientation, ethnicity, religion, and just about any other social and political category. Using critical inquiry in the classroom is a

---

*Contributed by Natalie Sekicky.

matter of creating a safe place for all students and then challenging them to consider and reconsider along with you the origins of traditions, stereotypes, and double standards that limit human growth. Teaching students to live critically and democratically is a matter of helping them learn to pay attention—to themselves and especially to others—and to feel outraged so that they can go on to construct a more just society. Practicing critical inquiry also means turning that scrutinizing and questioning eye on your own teaching and your own school so that you can better meet the needs of a diverse student population.

The exciting promise of teaching this way lured me out of newsrooms and into the classroom. As someone who grew up paying attention and feeling outraged (it must have been those Watergate Hearings I absorbed as a 4-year-old), I turned to journalism as a means of creating change in the world. I soon realized that by writing one story about sexual harassment, for example, I could not create as much change as I might by helping young people think critically about the effects of harassment in their own high school hallways. Writing one human interest story about a person who lives courageously with a disability is noble, but helping students rethink their habitual use of the word "retarded" to describe things they consider silly or inadequate promises greater change in societal attitudes. So, always attentive and often outraged, I teach high school students the ins and outs of journalism. Along the way, I share my critical capacities with them in an effort to help them develop their own. Together, we tackle some complex issues, such as gender stereotypes, racism, and homophobia. Based on feedback from students, I believe this critical approach to teaching has helped them construct some of the most meaningful learning of their school careers.

A dramatic example of teaching for critical awareness occurred in my classroom a few years ago. On that day, I posed this question to my students: *What criteria should journalists use to screen photographs for publication?* In the months leading up to that day, we had engaged in numerous conversations about ethics and journalism. My students were steadily developing critical capacities about newspapers and television news broadcasts. They debated the rationale for interviewing grieving relatives or traumatized victims of accidents or crimes. They questioned a local investigative reporter's practice of sabotaging his subjects on camera. They wondered why Cleveland journalists found so much to say and write about the city's pro sports teams and so little about everything else. They critiqued high school journalists who published humor that demeaned people. They struggled to discern between what people need to know and what they want the media to tell them.

Resting solidly on that foundation, we built up to the unique ethical questions that crop up in photojournalism. The students were learning how to design pages, and choosing strong photos that vividly illustrate stories is an important skill for designers. A few days before, I had found an excellent resource to prompt discussion of photo criteria. The *Cleveland Plain Dealer* had run a story on the front of its women's section about research on athletic performance and menstruation. (Why the newspaper has a women's section is yet another subject for critical inquiry. Where is the men's section? Oh, I see—all the rest of them.) The story referenced long-held beliefs that physical activity was unhealthy for women during menstruation, beliefs that led many high school girls to sit out of physical education classes over the years. The story not only contradicted those beliefs, but also indicated that some women's athletic performances are actually enhanced during menstruation. The story was accompanied by a color photograph of a female marathon runner breaking through the finish-line tape. She was sweaty, exhausted, and triumphant—and her legs were streaked with menstrual blood.

I immediately set that page aside for use in class because it promised compelling discussion about journalism standards. I also knew, after three years of teaching high school students, that few subjects silenced girls and rattled boys more than menstruation. As a high school student myself, the only references to menstruation I ever heard took the form of euphemisms from girls and assertions from boys that any female behavior they disliked was a byproduct of the offending female "PMS-ing." These linguistic schemes, designed to mask or stigmatize women's biology, angered me. When I took a women's studies course in college, I began to see them as part of a larger tradition that limited women's opportunities. (No need to take an angry woman seriously—she's just on the "rag.") Now, after years of outrage at such insults and ignorance, I had a tool that would help students address some important questions, first through a journalistic exercise and then as a critique of the social construction of gender.

After asking students to discuss what kinds of photographs are suitable for publication, I passed around the page bearing the photo of the marathon runner and asked students to consider whether they would publish that picture or one like it if presented with the chance. That's when the fun began.

One male student, a sophomore football player, was visibly disgusted and agitated. "We don't need to see that!" he exclaimed.

"See what?" I asked.

"THAT!" He pointed to the page I now held up for view.

"What?" I prodded. I wanted him to explain his decision, and I told him his explanation would be incomplete without specific language.

"We don't need to see that kind of blood!" he replied.

"What kind? Where does it come from?" I asked.

"From that place!" he snapped.

"What place?" a few girls asked.

The student couldn't answer. Not because he didn't know the answer, but because he had been socially conditioned never to speak about menstruation in an honest way.

"You can say uterus! It's not a dirty word!" some girls implored.

By now the room was buzzing. Other boys were attempting to explain their objections. A few girls were pressing them to make factual arguments and some quietly suggested that the blood was no different from the sweat on the runner. Other girls said nothing but were visibly engaged. Frustrations were building. Of course, I threw in some more fuel.

"What if our school newspaper ran a photo of a football player whose white uniform pants were streaked with blood?" I asked.

"That's different," came the quick male reply.

"How is it different?" a girl asked.

"Blood is blood, isn't it?" I asked. "And athletes who bleed show the physical price of sport, don't they?"

"That kind of blood is not OK! It's DIRTY!" the boy exclaimed, rising from his seat and overturning his desk in an effort to make his point.

At that point, everyone in the room knew we were immersed in a powerful learning experience. Students went on to discuss community values, prejudice, biology, double standards . . . . The conversation was dizzying. I urged the girls to consider why they had left most of the talking—and certainly the most aggressive talking—to the boys. After all, who knows more about menstruation? Girls responded that they rarely talk out loud about the subject, that they whisper instead. They went on to wonder why they felt compelled to do so and why their fathers and brothers voiced displeasure if asked to purchase tampons at the store. The class contemplated what historical sources lead people to think menstruation is dirty, what that assumption means for women, and how newspapers can help educate readers about false perceptions. When the bell sounded, the conversation continued as students filed out the door. The next day, they agreed that publishing that photograph was beneficial because it clearly illustrated the story and prompted an intense discussion of important gender issues.

Was it scary? Yes! I was a fourth-year teacher, but I was in my first year at a new school at the time of this event (and not yet tenured). Did I wonder if I would be hauled into a meeting once word of the day's events made it to 25 dinner tables across the city? Yes. Did I expect some backlash for introducing my feminist values into the discussion? Maybe. But I am committed to addressing discrimination in all its forms, especially sexism and homophobia. That commitment, I feel, ethically empowers me to help students think critically about the world, both inside and outside of school, even when the topics are controversial. Granted, when the class began, I had no idea the response from certain students would be so energetic; nor did I know one student would share so many extreme views. I could have shut down discussion and moved on to a less provocative example. However, the opportunity to take on a sexist standard arose; and the students and I elected to take it.

Now, two years later, students from that largely freshman and sophomore class have become editors of the school newspaper. They often speak of that day. They describe the photo, reenact the arguments, and marvel at boys' discomfort with something that is a regular part of girls' lives. They tell me they'll never forget it. And each year, new journalism students learn of the event from students who were there. They demand to see that photo and engage in their own critical analysis. I am thrilled by this response. In it, I recognize young people's ability to confront attitudes and practices that contribute to inequality. I challenge them to identify the foundations of their beliefs and to consider the power issues hidden in them. Who benefits when we make jokes about PMS? Whose interests are being served when we accept blood on some athletes but not on others? Who suffers when a fundamental aspect of women's biology is considered dirty? Whose lives are limited because of such attitudes? What can be done to alleviate those limitations?

I make time for conversations such as this one in spite of the pressing need to cover all the fundamentals of reporting, writing and editing stories, and designing pages. I do it because I consider such conversations crucial to my commitment to critical inquiry. These classroom exchanges are essential to teaching responsible, skillful journalism. I strongly believe that critical awareness is a key component of academic excellence in our society.

Opportunities for schoolwide action exist, as well; in such cases, knowledge of community and school values, politics, and power structures is essential. Again during my fourth year teaching (the first at a new school), paying attention to the morning announcements led to outrage. In an effort to boost attendance at an upcoming game, a senior member of the boys' lacrosse team made an announcement encouraging students to come to the contest. In his excitement, he promised that the lacrosse team would "send those fairies home crying." I don't always listen to the morning announcements, but I did that day. As a result, I found myself in a difficult situation. I was determined to see that anti-gay slur addressed by the adults in the school, especially after I noticed flyers for the game posted everywhere (even the main office door) and featuring a crudely drawn, winged portrayal of a fairy. On the other hand, as a new teacher who lacked tenure and political clout in the school, I was in a precarious position from which to intervene in a case of homophobia—one of the most sensitive topics in education.

Fueling my outrage in this instance was my knowledge of the school system's commitment to honoring diversity, a position mirrored in the community. Where was that commitment in the aftermath of the offensive announcement? By lunch time, I was ready to write an indignant letter to the principal. However, I first sought out other veteran teachers whom I knew were critically mindful. (It was as if we sought one another out; they were equally disturbed and ready to act.) Together, we formed a coalition and circulated a letter of protest that noted the apparent exclusion of gay and lesbian students and faculty from the district's concern for diversity. After many colleagues signed the letter, we took it to the principal with a request for action. As a result, the student wrote a letter of apology to the student newspaper; and with the endorsement of the principal, our coalition formed a gay-straight alliance to provide a safe atmosphere for all students to inquire about the impact of homophobia in school and society.

It's worth noting that many adults and students heard nothing unusual in the announcements that day. When I asked both groups what they thought of the "fairies" comment, many said, "I heard it, but I didn't think anything of it." In fact, the student who said it echoed those responses when I spoke with him about his choice of words. "I didn't mean it as gay," he told me. "I just meant, you know, sissy." Now, as an English teacher, should my interpretation of politically sensitive words like "fairy" be unquestioned? Certainly not. But as a teacher who practices critical inquiry, I pay attention to words like fairy and fag and dyke because I know those words are hateful expressions that repeatedly wound students and teachers—gay and straight—every day at school. (I pay special attention to them when they are spoken over the public address system without any critical response from school officials. What message does that send gay and lesbian students? Homophobia is school policy?) I doubt the student who inflicted those wounds in the name of team spirit ever understood the significance of his act. As I spoke with him about his unsportsmanlike attempt to bolster his team's chances by degrading his opponent and about the added injustice of using people's sexual orientation as the tool for that degradation, I sensed he lacked the critical capacities necessary to see the harm in his words. I can only hope that our brief conversation may eventually spark his attention.

The case of the lacrosse player raises an important question: *How do you become critically mindful? How do you develop critical capacities that will allow you to pay attention and ask the right questions so that you might teach for a more equitable society?* If the average student coming out of high school hasn't been taught to think about matters of race, gender, class, or sexual orientation, how can we expect teachers to suddenly snap into critical consciousness?

Like most people who choose to teach, I look back to my own teachers for inspiration. I had a few critically mindful teachers, and boy do I remember them. One was a sixth-grade teacher who chastised a boy who mercilessly teased another student for being "abnormal," a word he picked up somewhere and took great joy in applying to others. "Paul," she said sternly, "there's no such thing as normal!" She punctuated her point by smacking a magic marker against the wall. I can still see the green marks in my mind. I remember that incident nineteen years later because it was the first time I thought of one of my teachers as a hero. Her fierce defense of that student and her public assertion that no one had to live up to a fictional ideal stays with me to this day. In fact, I've used that line with my own students when they singled out peers for abnormal status based on appearance, intellect, behavior, or any other criteria. Anyone who wants to practice critical inquiry in the classroom can probably find some version of it in their own teacher memories.

Another avenue to critical awareness lies in examining your own life experience. My identity practically demands critical inquiry as a way of life. As a woman and a lesbian, I am keenly aware of the role that political power structures play in my personal and professional life. I know that these identities put me at risk of sexism, homophobia—even violence. Of course, every teacher's identity is unique. However, I'm sure most teachers know and love someone who is female, or gay, or African American, for example. To teach for a safer, more equitable society would benefit those friends and loved ones, too.

Perhaps the best motivation for practicing critical inquiry lies in the very responsibilities that every caring educator accepts. As a teacher, I am responsible for ensuring a safe learning environment for all of my students. I am obligated to treat every student with respect and to see to it students respect one another at school. I am charged with the duty of helping every student learn and grow so that he or she might be able to live democratically. Any teacher who takes on these duties holds the key to critical inquiry. I try to achieve these goals every day, and I do it by paying attention to my students and their individual identities. I do it by showing outrage when students are mistreated. I do it by striving to make sure no student fails to learn because the structure of school and society does not acknowledge his or her capacity or right to exist and to become his or her dream.

As a high school senior, I was approached by the superintendent of my school district. He asked what I hoped to study in college. When I confidently said, "I'm going to journalism school," his response fell short of the standard I hold for educators today.

"Journalism!" he scoffed. "You may as well just sell your body on the street."

Given that comment, it's probably no coincidence that I, a child of two teachers, chose to practice journalism with high school students and that I teach it with a critical consciousness. It's my hope that my students will never endure a similar insult, one that I took in silent grief. If they do hear it, I want them to pay attention and fire back.

I want them to live that bumper sticker.

REFERENCES

Aronowitz, S., & Giroux, H. (1985). *Education under siege.* South Hadley, MA: Bergin & Garvey.

Bartolome, L. I. (1995). Beyond the methods fetish: Toward a humanizing pedagogy. In G. C. Noya, K. Geismar, & G. Nicoleau

(Eds.), *Shifting histories: Transforming education for social change* (pp. 39–60). Cambridge, MA: Harvard Educational Review.

Cherryholmes, C. (1999). *Reading pragmatism.* New York: Teachers College Press.

Freire, P. (1987). Letter to North-American teachers. In I. Shor (Ed.), *Freire for the classroom* (pp. 211–214). Portsmouth, NH: Boynton & Cook.

Gove, P. B. (Ed.). (1986). *Webster's third new international dictionary of the English language.* Springfield, MA: Merriam-Webster.

Greene, M. (1986). Reflection and passion in teaching. *Journal of Curriculum and Supervision, 2,* 68–81.

Greene, M. (1988). *The dialectic of freedom.* New York: Teachers College Press.

Kanpol, B. (1998). *Teachers talking back and breaking bread.* Kreskill, NJ: Hampton Press.

Kincheloe, J. L. (1999). Critical democracy and education. In J. G. Henderson & K. R. Kesson (Eds.), *Understanding democratic curriculum leadership* (pp. 70–83). New York: Teachers College Press.

Ladson-Billings, G. (1994). *Dreamkeepers: Successful teachers of African-American children.* San Francisco: Jossey-Bass.

Lather, P. (1991). *Getting smart: Feminist research and pedagogy with/in the postmodern.* New York: Routledge.

Shor, I. (1993). Education is politics: Paulo Freire's critical pedagogy. In P. McLaren & P. Leonard (Eds.), *Paulo Freire: A critical encounter* (pp. 25–35). New York: Routledge.

Sirotnik, K. A. (1990). Society, schooling, teaching and preparing to teach. In J. I. Goodlad, R. Soder, & R. A. Sirotnik (Eds.), *The moral dimensions of teaching* (pp. 296–327). San Francisco: Jossey-Bass.

Sirotnik, K. A. (1991). Critical inquiry: A paradigm for praxis. In E. C. Short (Ed.), *Forms of curriculum inquiry* (pp. 243–258). Albany, NY: State University of New York Press.

Strike, K. A., & Soltis, J. F. (1985). *The ethics of teaching.* New York: Teachers College Press.

CHAPTER 7

TRANSFORMATIVE TEACHER LEADERSHIP

❦

"Appearances can be deceiving," Cameron Leder reminded me as we pulled into the parking lot. I knew what she meant. I certainly was not impressed with the rambling old building. Who would have ever imagined that we would come back to Barber School in the first place? We were successful in our current schools. We were tenured teachers with well-established classrooms and congenial working relationships with our fellow teachers and the principal. Cameron had a master's degree, and I (my name is Robin Sachem) had numerous graduate courses to my credit. We were placing ourselves in a vulnerable situation. Why? Why were we interviewing with a faculty team for positions in a center of inquiry school?

One reason was that we decided providing a better quality of educational services to our students meant more than maintaining the status quo—a familiar and apparently outwardly successful work routine. Yes, our students did well on standardized tests, and the community was generally pleased with our teaching. We were dissatisfied, however, with the isolated and fragmented nature of classroom teaching. We found it cumbersome to support each other's teaching inquiry in a setting where teaching and learning were maintained as individual endeavors. It was our sense that professional growth and student success depended on a school setting that encouraged time for dedicated study, planning, observation, and review, as well as a school culture that encouraged staff members to engage in this inquiry in a collaborative manner.

The interviews were the first clue that this truly was an extraordinary school. Since Cameron and I were applying to teach in the primary team, we were interviewed together. A team of primary-level staff members, including teachers, the librarian, the principal, student interns, and the parent resource coordinator, participated in the interview. Instead of the typical series of questions directed at a candidate by a principal with a team of teachers observing, the interview was more a conversation among all of us about schools as centers of inquiry. We talked about many ideas such as the role of public schools and teachers in a society with democratic ideals. We talked about ways we might make our classrooms a place where students experience a participatory democracy. We were asked to describe our personal sense of being called to the education profession and our views on caring and creative teaching. It was the most thoughtful dialogue about teaching and learning that I had ever been a part of. The primary team was clearly interested in our vision and the beliefs that guided our practice. At the conclusion of the interview, we were asked to share our view of teacher leadership. In preparation for the interviews, Cameron and I had prepared the following brief statement, which we read to the interview team:

> Collegial teacher leaders believe in the generative power of collaborative study. They believe that this study should support progressive decision making and should be a full expression of democratic ideals within the school setting. We recognize that teachers will study their practice in different ways, and we will be sure to celebrate these differences as long as all educational professionals are committed to a life of inquiry. We also recognize that support for collegial inquiry may require fundamental changes in a school's organizational structures.

Today, I am pleased to say Cameron and I are in our third year as teacher leaders at Barber School. Working in a teacher-initiated school-restructuring project has been a challenging, complex endeavor. We agree that the greatest challenge has been cultivating the professional relationships that support collaborative study. We co-construct curriculum, team teach, plan, enact the plan, observe and review together, organize schedules, interview potential interns, and serve as mentors to current interns. Teaching in a school that is organized to provide time for individual and collective reflection on practice enhances and sustains our professional development. We are guided by the insights and questions of our teammates, and we appreciate the sense of inquiry accountability that is developing in our school.

The teachers that originally established the vision for our school sought the commitment of the school district's administration to support professional growth for all faculty. The plan designates six percent of our school operating budget for continuing study. This money is managed by the faculty. It supports twenty percent of our time—the equivalent of one day per work week—for curriculum development work, teacher intern support (such as university student fieldwork and student teaching), and collegial inquiry activities. This time is made possible by including two teacher interns in our school's six teaching teams. With the support of veteran teachers, the interns take over a classroom, which enables the teacher to engage in professional development activities.

An important part of our professional development is dialogue about the quality of student work. In our many dialogues, we are able to share current research and raise questions for further inquiry about our teaching practices. Examples of student work inform our discussions as we share ideas and strategies for refining the quality of student work through the enhancement of our teaching practice. We understand the importance of inquiry artistry in teaching as we collectively struggle to become a school that practices our society's democratic ideals.

We have refined our professional inquiries in five different ways. As part of our ongoing efforts to improve our teaching craft, we collegially consider what it means to live a democratic life through **public moral inquiry.** By practicing **multiperspective inquiry,** we are open to diverse individual, community, and societal points of view about quality education. As much as possible, we try to integrate a caring and creative **deliberative inquiry** into our problem-solving activities. Through **autobiographical inquiry,** we explore the personal, aesthetic, and spiritual dimensions of our work. And, finally, we continually challenge one another to consider the consequences of our practices through **critical inquiry.** We collectively think about the ethical and political implications of our decision making and wonder if we are helping create a better society.

As we practice our professional inquiries, we allow for creative expression to influence our decisions about classroom practice. We look for ways to engage the imaginations of our students and colleagues and to encourage the development of our artistic becoming. We have found that the integration of art, music, drama, literature, poetry, and dance into the curriculum and the daily life of the school helps to develop our sensitive and creative energies.

As individuals, we bring our artistry into the setting of the learning community where we strive to create, re-create, and sustain our visions through collaborative problem-solving, dialogue, and the cultivation of community trust. We have grown beyond independence and self-reliance to the most empowering position of all: interdependence. This provides the safe environment needed to practice, to risk, and to grow.

As Cameron said, "Appearances can be deceiving."

INTRODUCTION

Chapter 1 began with the notion that teaching in a society with democratic ideals is a noble calling. We now return, full circle, to that idea. Consider the daunting global problems we face in the twenty-first century: the deep ecological wounding of our planet, the persistent possibility for nuclear war, and the degradation of oppressed peoples in an overpopulated world. To solve such major social problems, we must recognize that a reliance on science and technology will not be enough. We must find ways to cultivate our *loving intellect.* Educators must introduce their students to a life of generative and generous inquiry. They must teach for democratic living; and to teach in this way, they must cultivate their inquiry artistry. In short, they must integrate public moral inquiry, multiperspective inquiry, deliberative inquiry, autobiographical inquiry, and critical inquiry into their ongoing craft reflections.

Though teachers will decide to undertake this professional challenge in uniquely personal ways, their efforts will be both easier and more far-reaching if they work collaboratively with one another. For this to occur, the education profession will need the services of ***transformative teacher leaders.*** Transformative teacher leaders are educators who are deeply committed to their own journey of professional growth, eagerly participate in collaborative study activities with their colleagues, and willingly assume school reform responsibilities. Overall, they do whatever is necessary to encourage collegial inquiry at their individual schools.

TRANSFORMATIVE TEACHER LEADERSHIP

We now turn to an examination of three important features of transformative teacher leadership: (1) modeling professional transformation, (2) practicing collegial inquiry, and (3) assisting with school reform.

Modeling Professional Transformation

The capacity to create change begins, most fundamentally, with our own lives. While many think it grandiose to consider changing the world, others know that affecting small changes within our immediate circles of influence can have significant impact upon the lives of others. Ultimately, our capacity to effect change rests with our capacity to change our own lives.

Armstrong (1998) presents different ways that teachers can help students cultivate their talents. Calling this the awakening of personal "genius," he writes:

> The most powerful way to awaken genius in the classroom has nothing at all to do with lesson plans, classroom environment, learning materials, or instructional time. It has to do with you. And not you as an educator, but you as a human being. If you wish to spark the hidden light of genius in your students, you must first find and (re)light that spark in yourself. (p. 49)

Practicing the inquiry artistry presented in this book is one way to "awaken" your professional talents; and as you undertake your professional studies, you model disciplined inquiry learning for your students, their parents, and your colleagues.

Gershon and Straub (1989) describe the growing capacity to bring about change in one's life as "empowerment." This sense of self-agency rests on a deep confidence in one's ability to alter the environment for the better. In contrast, disempowered individuals believe that they cannot affect the quality of their lives. They experience an overriding sense of hopelessness and fatalism. Teachers, who are "awakening" to their inquiry capacities, function as empowered professionals who can inspire their colleagues. We are familiar with the journey of well-known mythical figures such as Odysseus in *The Odyssey,*

Dorothy in *The Wizard of Oz,* and Luke Skywalker in the *Star Wars* films. These characters undertake a hero or heroine's journey through very difficult circumstances. Because they are motivated by deep meaning and higher purpose, their mythic journeys inspire many others. Brown and Moffett (1999) draw a parallel between the hero and heroine's journey of discovery and educational reform:

> In effect, we are all heroes immersed in a quest to help our schools and school systems respond to the increasingly complex demands of the world of the Information Age. Old answers are no longer viable for the new questions we are confronting, just as old paradigms and old solutions are insufficient to respond to the new and unanticipated problems in contemporary education. We are all both individual and collaborative questors, searching for viable ways to transform our schools into communities of academic integrity, lifelong learning, and extraordinary caring for the children we serve. The object of our quest is the capacity to initiate, support, and sustain meaningful educational change. (p. 3)

Transformative teacher leaders are professionals who model this quest for others.

Practicing Collegial Inquiry

Transformative teacher leaders eagerly collaborate with their colleagues in a spirit of *collegial inquiry*. Professional collaboration should not be confused with congenial social relations. Sergiovanni (1990) notes that congeniality refers to "friendly human relationships and the development of strong, supportive social norms that are independent from the standards of the teaching profession and the purposes and work at school" (p. 119). When teachers talk about the weather, a local sports team, or any other nonprofessional topic, they are being congenial with one another. Only when their interactions have a professional focus can they be said to be collaborating.

Though collaboration can take place in many unique ways and in many different settings, teachers generally utilize five approaches: information exchanging, modeling, coaching, supervising, and mentoring. These five approaches can occur separately or in some combination, and they can involve differing levels of professional commitment.

Collaborative exchanging occurs when information is shared. This most often occurs when teachers swap techniques or strategies with one another. Classroom teachers within the context of a learning community might collaborate in this way when they are trying to assimilate new information in an efficient manner.

Collaborative modeling occurs when one professional demonstrates a teaching skill to one or more colleagues. This might occur in a professional development session where teachers are trying to understand a new instructional approach, or it might occur when a teacher invites a colleague to observe a lesson in the classroom for the purpose of demonstrating an innovative strategy.

Collaborative coaching refers to a relationship between two professionals in which one is more experienced than the other. This implies a relationship over a period of time. In this case, one teacher may engage in the process of helping a colleague by observing classroom practice and dialoguing with the other teacher about improving classroom instruction. Collaborative coaching is most helpful when one colleague approaches another on an informal basis to seek assistance with his or her own professional development. A positive school culture will encourage the risk taking that is necessary to engage in this type of collaboration.

Collaborative supervising occurs when a more experienced colleague provides evaluative feedback to one or more colleagues. This approach is different from collaborative coaching in that it involves a judgmental relationship. Otherwise, it is very much like the process of collaborative coaching.

Collaborative mentoring describes a long-term relationship between two professionals in which one has more experience than the other. A mentor attempts to provide guidance on all aspects of a teacher's professional life. Mentoring is, therefore, a highly personal and supportive form of collaboration. During the entry year of teaching, many school districts provide a mentor teacher. If your school district does not provide collaborative support in this manner, you may want to request it.

Collaborative exchanging, modeling, coaching, supervising, and mentoring may or may not be infused with a spirit of *collegial inquiry.* Collegial inquiry only occurs when everyone involved feels that his or her professional empowerment has been enhanced. There must be a deep respect for each person's unique inquiry needs, style, and developmental journey. When the collaborations lack this sense of professional *reciprocity,* collegial inquiry is not being practiced.

Assisting with School Reform

Transformative teacher leaders work with key administrators, primarily their principals, to change their schools into inquiry learning communities. Because they understand that significant school reform cannot take place without teachers' active support, transformative teacher leaders view educational leadership through a collegial lens. Lambert (1998) writes:

> When we equate "leadership" with "leader", we are immersed in a "trait theory": If only a leader possessed these certain traits, we would have good leadership. This tendency has caused those who might have rolled up their sleeves and pitched in to help to abstain from the work of leadership, thereby abdicating both their responsibilities and their opportunities. Although leaders do perform acts of leadership, a separation of the concepts can allow us to reconceptualize leadership itself. (p. 5)

Transformative teacher leaders "reconceptualize" leadership in Lambert's terms. They understand that teachers must assume responsibility for their own professional fates and that *quality of work life* is a very important occupational issue—as important as salary and benefits.

Though the specifics of how transformative teacher leaders can best support school reform depend on particular institutional circumstances, several general areas of professional responsibility can be identified:

- Working with others to envision schools as inquiry learning communities
- Establishing collegial staff development
- Practicing teacher-centered curriculum development

§ Encouraging collaboration between teachers and other direct service providers

§ Creating respect for responsible diversity

§ Altering power relationships and organizational structures

§ Seeking broad collegial relations

§ Providing local policy leadership within the school and between the school and the neighboring community

It is not easy for many educational stakeholders, including teachers and their students, students' parents, school administrators, community leaders, and local citizens, to envision schools as inquiry learning communities. A retired teacher notes this problem:

> I have been disturbed for some time by the suggestion that public schools be modeled after a factory's method of operation. I am just as concerned that the schools be compared to a business. The schools are neither. The school is not a factory, because it does not produce "widgets." Widgets are made for very specific uses and according to precise specifications so that they may be interchangeable in all widget workings. The school is not a business because the school is not a profit-seeking enterprise. The outcomes from schooling do not benefit its stockholders monetarily. As a retired teacher, may I suggest the analogy of a greenhouse. In a greenhouse, products are not manufactured, but living things are nurtured. In a greenhouse, the environment is optimal for the development of the frail, injury-prone and precious living things. It is invigorating and stimulating and free from harm. In a greenhouse, the living things are provided with individual requirements. Some need more water, some need different food, some need more light. . . . In a greenhouse, the results of growth are varied. (Roberto, 1999)

Adapting Roberto's "greenhouse" metaphor, schools can be viewed as community institutions where minds are *grown*. Eisner (1994) writes that the "mind unlike [the] brain, which is a biological given, is a form of cultural achievement" and that schools "are cultures for creating minds" (p. x). In terms of the philosophical orientation of this book, schools can be viewed as places that cultivate *loving intellects;* and what is effective for a factory or a business may not be effective for a "greenhouse" of growing minds—for an inquiry learning community. Working with other educational stakeholders, transformative teacher leaders encourage and promote this fundamental shift in thinking about the nature of schooling.

Transformative teacher leaders encourage collegial staff development. They understand that the responsibility for professional development must, ultimately, be in the hands of empowered teachers. Traditionally, staff development has been the prerogative of school administrators without much input from teachers. Transformative teacher leaders work to change this arrangement. They help administrators reassess the process by which staff development is planned, enacted, and evaluated. Because they know that teachers cultivate their inquiry capacities in their own unique ways, they work with administrators to establish a wide range of formal and informal collaborative study opportunities through the flexible use of staff development time, money, and resources.

Transformative teacher leaders encourage curriculum development that is centered on teachers and their students. They understand that prepackaged educational programs and publishers' textbooks may not best meet the needs of their particular inquiry learning community, at least without significant adaptations. Therefore, they seek ways to initiate and support school-based curriculum collaborations. Henderson and Hawthorne (2000) provide detailed guidance on how this can occur. They use a music metaphor to describe this curriculum work: "We advocate a complex form of curriculum leadership involving a diverse group of people working in overlapping classroom, school, and community contexts. Imagine a jazz combo composed of creative, improvisational musicians interacting with one another to create compelling music, and you get the idea of what we are trying to facilitate in this book" (p. 2). Transformative teacher leaders are active participants in this school-site "jazz combo."

Transformative teacher leaders see their professional role in very broad terms and encourage their colleagues to work in the same way. They willingly work outside the classroom and the school. They seek ways to collaborate with direct service providers in order to coordinate services that best meet the needs of children and their families. This might involve the services of school psychologists, social workers, community health professionals, physicians, and/or therapists. They understand that when school personnel and direct service providers share information, all parties—particularly the students—benefit. Students receiving special education services need the support of an educational team adept at coordinating the work of many service providers. School psychologists, physical and occupational therapists, speech pathologists, and guidance counselors are all an important part of this delivery system. Transformative teacher leaders encourage these diverse collaborative endeavors.

Transformative teacher leaders foster tolerance for diversity. They know that when human idiosyncrasy is treated as an asset, educational work can be more caring, creative, and passionate. They welcome diverse perspectives because they understand that distinctive beliefs, learning styles, and personalities, as well as broader gender, race, and ethnic differences, all contribute to the richness of an inquiry learning community. Zohar (1997) writes:

> The [highly energized] organization will thrive on diversity. The old vision of one truth, one way, one expression of reality, one best way of doing things, the either-or of absolute, unambiguous choice must give way to a plural way of accommodating the multiplicities and diversities of societies, markets, and individuals. Either-or must make way for both-and. "My way" must give way to shared vision, shared opportunity, and shared responsibility that recognize the validity of many paths from A to Z. As Einstein said, there are as many perspectives on the universe as there are observers, and each adds something. (p. 125)

Transformative teacher leaders share Zohar's deep respect for human diversity.

Transformative teacher leaders seek ways to collaboratively examine the power relationships and organizational structures that inhibit the emergence of, and support for, an inquiry learning community. Because they function as empowered professionals, they understand the importance of reciprocal power relations. They have the willingness and the ability to challenge those systems and structures that wield power over others

(Kreisberg, 1992). Educational structures have traditionally been designed to foster "top-down" power relations. Administrators make decisions that are implemented by teachers and other direct service providers. There is little or no opportunity for shared decision making. This management orientation is based on the belief that uniformity of opinion and action is the most effective way to run an organization. Transformative teacher leaders challenge this belief because they want to see schools transformed into inquiry learning communities. They want schools to become places that cultivate *loving intellects,* and they are willing to challenge all policies and practices that prevent this from happening. They agree with Zohar (1997) that "top-down hierarchies and structures . . . waste the creative, spontaneous resources of the quantum [the multifaceted, infinitely capable] self" (p. 125).

Transformative teacher leaders seek ways to influence others beyond the walls of the classroom or the school. They may choose to work on a district-level curriculum project or a policy-making committee. They may become involved in state or national professional organizations. They may find opportunities to attend professional conferences where teacher leaders are able to share their ideas with others in a context of informal discussions or more formal presentations. They may publish their experiences in supportive professional journals and magazines. Whatever their leadership choices, they view their work in broad professional terms. They feel they are part of a larger educational *collegium,* and they seek ways to meaningfully interact with their fellow colleagues.

Finally, transformational teacher leaders understand the importance of creating a local policy environment that supports the emergence of schools as inquiry learning communities. They are willing to become involved in school-community politics, and they seek opportunities to dialogue with influential local and state legislators. Because they know that many parents and other educational stakeholders view themselves as educational experts, they seek ways to foster community dialogue on the role of public education in a society with democratic ideals. In the United States, town meetings and other public forums were instituted to facilitate community decision making. Transformational teacher leaders adapt such strategies to their professional purposes (Henderson and Kesson, 1999). They actively pursue and cultivate community support for the transformation of schools into inquiry learning communities.

TRANSFORMATIVE TEACHER LEADERSHIP SCAFFOLDING

You need not wait until you are a well-established professional before thinking about becoming a transformative teacher leader. You can begin thinking about this topic at any point in your career. Therefore, we have placed the guiding questions in this chapter along an "experiential continuum" that begins early in life and ends with retirement.

§ *Educational experiences prior to professional coursework.* Think back over your classroom experiences as a student. Can you identify a particular class or school setting that exemplifies any of the characteristics of a school as a center of inquiry? What activities and behaviors made these characteristics evident to you as a student? Which of the five forms of inquiry do you see evident in the lived experiences of students, staff, and parents? Pursue your own awakening.

§ *Early preservice fieldwork in conjunction with professional coursework.* These field experiences will give you the opportunity to observe and respond to some of the qualities and characteristics of a learning organization. Keep a reflective journal of your observations. Ask to attend staff meetings as an observer. Note the effective communication techniques used by the staff members to promote open, honest dialogue around school issues. Try to develop your own description of the beliefs that might be influencing their deliberations. Pursue your continual awakening.

§ *Concluding preservice fieldwork as a student teacher or intern.* During your student teaching or internship, work toward developing a collegial relationship with your cooperating teacher. Promote discussion of how collegial relationships are fostered and sustained in the particular school culture. If you are part of a teaching team, extend yourself and work to build your collaborative skills with the other members of the team. Note what specific actions and behaviors connote collegiality to you as well as to your teammates. Ask your cooperating teacher to offer reflections about your strengths in establishing collegial relationships. Pursue your continual awakening.

§   *Teaching in the first four years.* The induction year of teaching is usually so intense that you may not think you have the time to pursue collegial relationships. However, establish a relationship with at least one significant colleague. This will help support your continuing development. Focus on your interpersonal skills for open, honest dialogue about teaching. During the second and third years, try to expand your network of colleagues. Consider establishing or joining a professional study group. Keeping in mind the five forms of inquiry, begin to consider the ways in which your individual and collective inquiry might grow. Pursue your continual awakening and begin to look for ways to influence others to do the same.

§   *Teaching from the fourth to the sixth year.* By now, you may have developed an expansive repertoire of instructional practices. You have elevated your understanding of individual and collective inquiry. Are you prepared to extend yourself and welcome a student teacher or intern into your teaching setting? This will provide you with an opportunity to reexamine your own experiences and beliefs as you open yourself to the examination of your teaching practices by another. Can you begin to undertake any of the transformative teacher leadership responsibilities? Are you influencing others to live an inquiring, awakening life?

§   *Teaching from the seventh year to retirement.* Are you the teacher envisioned by your novice self a few years ago? What colleagues have been key factors in your professional development? What is the focus of your inquiry now? Have you continued your formal education in graduate school? Have you intentionally changed your job or school assignment to work in a situation more in tune to your beliefs? Are you now able to view yourself in one of the ways described in this chapter? Are you initiating inquiry within the learning community and participating in collective inquiry with staff, parents, and students? Are you looking for ways to expand your influence past the learning community to the larger community of your profession, or your city or town?

CONCLUDING COMMENTS

This book encourages you to view teaching as a vocation or calling, not as a job with a long summer vacation. You have been asked to consider the higher purposes of education in societies with democratic ideals and to undertake an arduous journey of *inquiry artistry*. All societies have individuals who encourage change because they envision a better life. Dr. Martin Luther King was such a person. Have you ever pondered what factors caused Dr. King to embrace his calling to improve the quality of life for *all* of his fellow citizens? What motivated him? Can you imagine educators teaching for democratic living? Can you imagine schools functioning as inquiry learning communities that nurture the *loving intellects* of their students? What impact could such teachers and such schools have on their society? If a passionate individual like Dr. King can make a difference, what could legions of public educators do?

When educators teach for democratic living, they encourage the development of the visionary or prophetic voice in each of their students. Spehler and Slattery (1999) link the development of this voice to the development of the inner life:

> The prophet is one who calls and inspires others to attend to matters of great significance. The development of the prophetic voice is a process involving psychological, spiritual, cognitive, and emotional aspects of our being. This process of evoking vision in others is very much dependent on an inner awakening, a realization of a personal capacity to perceive and impact the future. (p. 7)

As educators, we can impact future generations by preparing students to live a life of inquiry guided by democratic ideals. As children wrestle with pressing personal and social difficulties, we can allow them the time and space to inquire into their own very real problems. We can strengthen their belief in a future full of possibility, not one of cynicism and despair. When we educate in this way, students directly experience the challenges of living a life of inquiry within a community, and they learn that such a way of living takes time, patience, discipline, inner strength, and commitment.

As educators, our ability to make a *quality* difference in the lives of our students begins with the cultivation of our own inquiry capacities. In chapter 1, we acknowledged that the *inquiry artistry* presented in this book is a very high professional standard. Though it is quite demanding, we hope you are inspired by the challenge. Though this developmental journey is highly personal, we hope that you can find ways to collaborate with other professionals. Perhaps, you will even be able to work with colleagues on the transformation of your school into an inquiry learning community. We hope so. Envision a society where all of its public education institutions functioned as inquiry learning communities. Imagine the quality of life in that society.

Teacher Narrative*

When I was asked to make a contribution to this book on the topic of transformative teacher leadership, I was both flattered and surprised. After much personal reflection, I began to dialogue with other colleagues. It was through their comments that I learned that I was viewed as a teacher leader. It is obvious to me now that my passion for the educational process has affected my peers in ways that I was not aware. It is from this passion that I naturally share my philosophy, ideals, techniques, strategies, and knowledge of research-based practices. It is this passion for teaching that continually challenges me to constantly inquire by reading professional journals, by enrolling in university classes, and by implementing new strategies, techniques, and research-based programs in my classroom.

My educational journey began when I left the business world to pursue a career in early childhood education. I felt a calling to the teaching profession. I decided to return to school to complete a de-

---

*Contributed by Carol Chiorian.

gree in early childhood education. I was fortunate to be placed in a lab school setting located on a college campus. I began as a volunteer, did my student teaching in the center, then was employed as a lead teacher. We implemented practices that were being taught in the college classroom. We were shadowed by preservice teachers. Lessons were planned and implemented in collaborative teams. While teaching, we engaged the learning community in reflection on the children, the teachers, and the lessons. It was here that I realized that my own personal educational experiences as a child conflicted with what I was learning and observing in the early childhood classroom. I was educated in an authoritarian school setting where we were given worksheets, used a basal reader, and memorized mathematical procedures. Upon reflection, I see that my introduction to inquiry-based learning began in this preschool setting when I studied and observed how children learn. It was in this atmosphere that I realized the importance, the effectiveness, and the satisfaction of being part of a learning community. It was here that my own personal transformation began.

When I entered public education, I felt isolated because, for the first time, I was teaching, planning, and assessing students independently in a self-contained classroom. Interaction and collaborative time with my peers, as well as dialogue about philosophy, vision, and inquiry was limited or nonexistent due to the physical structure of the school combined with a lack of sufficient planning and collaborative time. However, teachers were willing to share worksheets, art projects, and classroom management techniques. It appeared to me that the educational process had not changed since I had attended school. This created a feeling of dissonance because I knew I had been transformed to an educator who believed that children construct their understandings, that diversity is necessary for inquiry, and that one of my goals is to inspire students to believe they are lifelong learners. I began to seek out colleagues who shared my passion and commitment. Fortunately, I found two colleagues who were experiencing the same feelings. We began to dialogue about philosophy, curriculum, learning, and best practices for children. We realized we shared a discomfort with the learning model we were using to teach science and social studies. This dissonance and discomfort was the springboard from which we began our collaborative group.

We were teaching science, social studies, and health units in a rotation system that was in place prior to our arrival at the school. We were each assigned certain units, and we would teach them to nine different classes. We would have our students for only one rotation, then our students would rotate to the other eight teachers. This philosophy conflicted with our beliefs about how children learn. Since collaboration and dialogue were not institutional priorities, our attempts to implement changes were met with resistance and skepticism. Dialogue about these uncomfortable issues was difficult and painful for the staff. As always, change takes time; and it was not until a year later that we were able to form a collaborative team of six teachers who shared the same philosophies and practices. I believe this was a starting point for the entire staff to begin to reflect on philosophies and to begin to dialogue about the rotation system. However, the staff was still not ready to begin an inquiry journey as a learning community.

As a small collaborative team, we created a climate of collegial inquiry. We were each growing individually and as a team. Even though we were a small collaborative team, we inadvertently isolated our philosophies and practices from the remaining staff. We should have invited others into our collaborative group. It was not until a tragedy hit the group that we realized how isolated we had made ourselves. My closest colleague and team teacher was diagnosed with a terminal illness. She took a medical retirement during the second week of school. Because we shared philosophies, lessons, and mostly a passion for our work, her loss impacted me greatly. I no longer felt a part of the collaborative team. I felt alone with no one to share my passion.

Sometime later, I was invited by the assistant superintendent to participate in a teacher leadership class. I was honored to be considered a leader and readily accepted her offer. Our first class met in October and I was not sure what the class would entail. We were to meet five times during the school year and conduct an action research project in our schools using our leadership skills. I was introduced to new terms such as postmodern education, inquiry learning, and transformative teacher leadership. We discussed teaching for democratic living, constructivism, inquiry, reflective teaching, and professional artistry. We dialogued about our deep beliefs, our vision, and social justice. I felt invigorated and renewed by the dialogue. I felt comfortable sitting in a classroom with others who shared my passion.

The action research project was not difficult to identify. I was on appraisal that year and I needed to formulate job targets. Naturally, one of my targets became my action research project. I had completed one when I worked on my master's degree. It was here that I learned that teachers study the research of others as well as become researchers themselves. My research project would consist of researching teacher leadership, reflective inquiry, dialogue, collaboration, and decision making. This was a perfect forum for me to be able to share my enthusiasm and passion with the entire staff. The time had come to open dialogue in order to become a more thoughtful professional community. With the support of my principal, a strong proponent of transformative teacher leadership, we would have the staff reflect on our vision and mission statements and dialogue about how we inquire and make decisions. My ultimate goal was to bring the staff together to begin dialogue, inquiry, and reflection about the science, social studies, and health rotation system.

We began our inquiry journey as the entire staff read the book *Awakening Genius in the Classroom* by Armstrong (1998). We read and discussed the book over three consecutive staff meetings. We were invited to bring pillows, sit on the floor, and just enjoy the reading. We then met in small groups and openly engaged in self-examinations on how our individual "genius" had been shut down. This process opened the door to the importance of professional inquiry.

I was inspired by Armstrong's book. He stated many of my strong beliefs. He discusses how important it is for us to reawaken the genius in ourselves. He writes:

> Simply being aware of what fills your life with the greatest interest and passion can help launch this search. Sometimes it can be helpful to remember your dreams for clues about what fills you with energy and excitement, or to remember your own childhood and adolescence, when you might have been passionately involved in hobbies, arts, or other activities that you've neglected over the years. (Armstrong, 1998, p. 51)

My dreams and passions were awakened when I taught preschool, and I held fast to those passions and knew I could implement them in my elementary classroom.

I began reading books by Parker Palmer, Thomas Sergiovanni, Linda Lambert, and James Henderson on teacher leadership and reflective inquiry. My principal supported my efforts by sharing her books with me and encouraging me to dialogue with her about my readings. She then organized a small group of teachers who volunteered to research the decision-making process in our building. We discussed collaborative action research. We listed and discussed questions that we would like to have researched. We ended the year by beginning. We are beginning to collaborate and inquire. We are beginning to reflect on our practices. We are beginning to move from craftsmanship to professional artistry. I am still continuing the research today. I have just begun the journey of teacher leadership and I am still working on my action research project.

Because of the manner in which my beliefs impact and drive my practices, I have apparently been perceived by my peers and the administration as a transformative teacher leader. What is important to me is not the fact that I am viewed in this way, but that I continue to inquire, reflect, and practice my deep beliefs about education and children. It is important that I help students experience democracy as a way of life and that I continually nurture my inquiry artistry.

I have learned that education is a journey for the teacher, as well as the student. It takes years of reflection and inquiry to match your practices with your passion. It takes time and effort to bring about a collaborative atmosphere. That part of the journey is all about learning to respect differences in philosophy and practice while continuing to work on the creation of an inquiry learning community. It is a combination of all of the above that makes teaching a professional art.

It was through the reflective process of writing this narrative that I became more aware of my journey toward professional artistry. It was through my personal reflection, inquiry, and dialogue that I have come to realize that my personal goal is to teach for democratic living. I believe that it will be through collegial inquiry that this goal will be achieved. As a staff, we have just begun the necessary dialogue and collaborative decision making. Through our continued collegial efforts, I envision us collectively integrating inquiry artistry into our daily lives. We are beginning to engage in public moral inquiry, multiperspective inquiry, deliberative inquiry, self-inquiry, and critical inquiry together.

It is important for me to recognize two colleagues who have supported and encouraged me. In the spirit of collaboration, I would like to thank Nancy Bronchetti, who aided me in writing this personal narrative, for her support, trust, and belief in me as a transformative teacher leader. I would also like to thank Mary Reed Curtin, my soul mate, for always inspiring me and sharing my passion for teaching. I would also like to thank Kathleen Dickinson whose professional opinion I seek and admire.

REFERENCES

Armstrong, T. (1998). *Awakening genius in the classroom.* Alexandria, VA: Association for Supervision and Curriculum Development.

Brown, J. L., & Moffett, C. A. (1999). *The hero's journey: How educators can transform schools and improve learning.* Alexandria, VA: Association for Supervision and Curriculum Development.

Eisner, E. W. (1994). *Cognition and curriculum reconsidered* (2nd ed.). New York: Teachers College Press.

Gershon, D., & Straub, G. (1989). *Empowerment: The art of creating your life as you want it to be.* New York: Dell.

Henderson, J. G., & Hawthorne, R. D. (2000). *Transformative curriculum leadership* (2nd ed.). Upper Saddle River, NJ: Merrill/Prentice Hall.

Henderson, J. G., & Kesson, K. R. (Eds.). (1999). *Understanding democratic curriculum leadership.* New York: Teachers College Press.

Kreisberg, S. (1992). *Transforming power: Domination, empowerment, and education.* Albany, NY: State University of New York Press.

Lambert, L. (1998). *Building leadership capacity in schools.* Alexandria, VA: Association for Supervision and Curriculum Development.

Roberto, J. W. (1999, September 12). Voice of the people. *Akron Beacon Journal.*

Sergiovanni, T. J. (1990). *Value-added leadership: How to get extraordinary performance in schools.* Orlando, FL: Harcourt Brace Jovanovich.

Spehler, R., & Slattery, P. (1999). Voices of imagination: The artist as prophet in the process of social change. *International Journal of Leadership in Education, 2* (1), 1–11.

Zohar, D. (1997). *Rewiring the corporate brain.* San Francisco: Berrett-Koehler.

APPENDIX

THE TEACHER-CHARACTER IDEOLOGICAL MAP

IDEOLOGICAL OVERVIEW

The creation of the four teacher-characters for this book emerges from a synthesis of two systems of ideological analysis. One system was created by Bernier and Williams (1973a) for the purpose of studying the ideological foundations of educational practice in the United States. Bernier (1981) summarizes their system as follows:

> Williams and I, in our analysis of the ideological foundations of American education, identified six major belief systems which give direction to education in the United States. In each case, a teacher model was suggested to illustrate the way in which these ideologies are activated in schools. The belief systems identified and their teacher models are: Scientism—behavior modifier; Romanticism—artist; Puritanism—moral exemplar; Progressivism—facilitator; Nationalism—patriot or ethnic exemplar; Educationism—professional. (p. 297)

The other system of ideological analysis is an adaptation of Kliebard's (1986) study of the American educational curriculum between 1893 and 1958. According to Kliebard, this sixty-five-year time span represents a period "when curriculum reform emerged from somewhat tentative beginnings to become a national preoccupation" (p. xiii). Kliebard identifies four ideological traditions, and his analysis has been adapted to the study of teacher education by Zeichner and Liston (1991). Zeichner and Liston identify four fundamental traditions of good teaching: academic, social efficiency, developmentalist, and social reconstructionist. Because Zeichner and Liston directed their work specifically toward the study of teaching, their ideological analysis will be presented first. The four teacher-character ideologies will then be briefly discussed with reference to both Zeichner and Liston's and Bernier and Williams' analytical systems.

ZEICHNER AND LISTON'S SYSTEM

Academic Tradition

In Zeichner and Liston's (1991) ideological map, academics argue that good teachers are liberal arts scholars and subject matter specialists, who can facilitate students' disciplined-based inquiries. They help students become conversant with the great ideas of Western civilization. Hutchins (1952) summarizes the liberal education goals of academic teachers as follows:

> The liberally educated man [sic] understands, by understanding the distinctions and interrelations of the basic fields of subject matter, the differences and connections between poetry and history, science and philosophy, theoretical and practical science; he understands that the same methods cannot be applied in all these fields; he knows the methods appropriate to each. The liberally educated man comprehends the ideas that are relevant to the basic problems and that operate in the basic fields of subject matter. He knows what is meant by soul, state, God, beauty, and by other terms that are basic to the discussion of fundamental issues. He has some notion of the insights that these ideas, singly or in combination, provide concerning human experience. (pp. 3–4)

Social Efficiency Tradition

Social efficiency advocates believe that good teachers should follow the guidelines established by scientific studies of educational practices. These studies follow a three-part logic:

1. Based on a study of society's social and economic needs, decide on appropriate learning achievement objectives for students. These will be the desired quality outcomes or "products" of effective teaching.

2. Using valid experimental procedures, examine efficient instructional methods or "processes" for achieving these educational products.

3. Use the results of this research to identify important instructional competencies to be practiced in teacher education programs.

After providing a comprehensive literature review of this process-product research, Brophy and Good (1986) write:

> The myth that teachers do not make a difference in student learning has been refuted, and programmatic research reflecting the description-correlation-experimentation loop . . . has begun to appear. As a result, the fund of available information on producing student achievement . . . has progressed from a collection of disappointing and inconsistent findings to a small but well-established knowledge base that includes several successful field experiments. (p. 370)

Developmentalist Tradition

To developmentalists, good teachers practice a child-centered instruction that is based on the study of students' maturational levels and learning interests. Zeichner and Liston (1991) describe the two-year Developmental Teacher Education Program at the University of California at Berkeley, a graduate program designed in accordance with this ideological frame of reference:

> This program . . . is guided by the view that understanding of developmental principles is the best preparation for teaching. Students are exposed in their courses to theories of cognitive, social, moral, and language development and then focus in various practicums on the application of developmental principles to the teaching of mathematics, science, and literacy. (p. 12)

Social Reconstructionist Tradition

To social reconstructionists, good teachers address the real problems of social injustice in their educational practices. They want to engage in specific emancipatory learning projects because they believe that education is an important avenue for sociocultural reform. Freire (1970/1971) articulates this goal:

> Education as the practice of freedom—as opposed to education as the practice of domination—denies that man [sic] is abstract,

isolated, independent, and unattached to the world; it also denies that the world exists as a reality apart from men. Authentic reflection considers neither abstract man nor the world without men, but men in their [problematic] relations with the world.

. . . Problem-posing education, as a humanist and liberating praxis, posits as fundamental that men [sic] subjected to domination must fight for their emancipation. To that end, it enables teachers and students to become Subjects of the educational process by overcoming authoritarianism and an alienating intellectualism; it also enables men to overcome their false perception of reality. The world . . . becomes the object of that transforming action by men which results in their humanization. (pp. 69, 74)

IDEOLOGIES OF THE TEACHER-CHARACTERS

The four teacher-characters have been given names and symbols denoting their ideological frame of reference.

Johnny Jackson advocates Zeichner and Liston's (1991) academic belief system. His symbol is an open book, standing for the love of great ideas.

Amy Nelson represents Zeichner and Liston's (1991) social efficiency perspective. This teaching ideology is based on the authors' application of scientism to educational practices. According to Bernier and Williams (1973a), *scientism* is the belief "that reality is or can be rationally controlled by man [sic] and that such an ordering implies predictability through the empirical testing of phenomenon by methods designed to secure objectivity and control" (p. 66). Amy Nelson's symbol is the personal computer, denoting efficient information processing, rational control, and economic achievement.

The third teacher-character is Dennis Sage, and his personal symbol is a teacher clasping the hand of a student, standing for his faith in the power of personal relationships. Dennis is a creative developmentalist, representing a synthesis of Zeichner and Liston's (1991) discussion of the developmentalist tradition and Bernier and Williams's (1973a) analysis of *romanticism,* which they describe as follows:

Romanticism is the ideology of the rebel. It is reflected in the life style and value system of the prophet, the visionary, the bohemian, the cynical philosopher, the vagabond, and the disen-

chanted bourgeois. It necessitates a demand for critical disaf-
filiation, for romanticists reject all *imposed* restrictions and standards. Romanticists are rugged individualists, especially in the
realm of ethics, and they are uncompromising and often vocif-
erous in their demand for the right of self-expression. In re-
jecting all external commandments, they rely upon their imagination and intuition in their search for truth. (p. 128)

The fourth teacher-character is Silvia Rivera, and her symbol
is the scales of justice. She represents Zeichner and Liston's (1991)
social reconstructionism, a teaching ideology that is further am-
plified by Bernier and Williams's (1973a) analysis of *puritanism:*

Puritanism views man [sic] holistically and from a moralistic
perspective. It is an ideology which combines the spiritual, aesthetic, and social aspects of man into a politico-economic
framework. Viewing man as a moral agent regardless of his role
in society and holding him accountable for all of his actions, it
demands integration of the human personality. (p. 230)

Bernier and Williams's (1973a) system of analysis also includes nationalism, progressivism, and educationism. One dimension of *nationalism,* the affirmation of nation-state patriotism,
is tacitly incorporated into the teacher-character's opinions. They
all function as Americans, though they draw on the work of people from other countries. Silvia Rivera also operates from a particular ethnic identity. As Bernier and Williams (1973a) argue, this
is another aspect of nationalism possessing deep historical roots:

In a general fashion, Nationalism may be viewed as an ideological thrust within a cultural community, a nationality, to
achieve a degree of social and/or political autonomy (e.g., various forms of Afro-Americanism such as Black Pride, Black
Capitalism, or Black Separatism), or as an ideological matrix
within a political community, a nation-state, designed to
achieve cultural homogeneity (e.g., the "melting-pot" type of
assimilation which was utilized to characterize the United
States in the heyday of immigration). (p. 239)

As Silvia Rivera explains in chapter 3, she was born in Puerto
Rico in 1961 and takes pride in her Puerto Rican/Hispanic identity. She believes in the American ideal of equal opportunity for

all. However, she thinks that this ideal must be reinterpreted for social groups that, in broad historical terms, have experienced oppression. She argues that equality of opportunity means different things to different people. For example, she believes that the principle of educational equity requires teachers to be sensitive to Hispanic students' culturally unique learning styles. She thinks it is not fair to treat first-generation Puerto Rican students the same as fourth-generation Irish students. Due to her views, she is a strong advocate of multiculturalism in education.

All four teacher-characters express progressivist and educationist sentiments. Collectively, they are committed to their continuing education. They all accept the challenge of *inquiry artistry* as presented in this book. In their own unique ways, they are all "progressive" in their professional outlook. Bernier and Williams (1973b) provide this overview of educational *progressivism:*

> Adhering to the old adage that moderation is the mother of virtue, progressivists dismiss both the rigid formalism of Puritanism and the rebellious individualism of Romanticism. They believe that Puritanism borders on tyranny, Romanticism on anarchy. Questions of value and ethical decisions may be open to individual response, but choices must be made within the social context with careful consideration given to the consequences of one's decision. Because man [sic] is by nature a social animal, the progressivists assert, the consequences of an individual's actions often affect other individuals. For this reason many decisions should be group decisions. (pp. 201–202)

The four teacher-characters are also advocates of *educationism,* or the belief in the professionalization of teaching. They all believe "that schooling influences positively the development of an individual's potential" (Bernier and Williams, 1973a, p. 340) and that teachers need to continuously cultivate their own professional growth to be the best possible facilitators of their students' growth. As advocates of teacher inquiry, they all concur with Barth's (1990) point: "Those who value . . . education, those who hope to improve our schools, should be worried about the stunted growth of teachers. Teacher growth is closely related to pupil growth" (p. 49).

REFERENCES

Barth, R. S. (1990). *Improving schools from within: Teachers, parents, and principals can make the difference.* San Francisco: Jossey-Bass.

Bernier, N. R. (1981). Beyond instructional context identification— Some thoughts for extending the analysis of deliberate education. In J. L. Green & C. Wallat (Eds.), *Ethnography and language in educational settings* (pp. 291–302). Norwood, NJ: Ablex.

Bernier, N. R., & Williams, J. E. (1973a). *Beyond beliefs: Ideological foundations of American education.* Upper Saddle River, NJ: Prentice Hall.

Bernier, N. R., & Williams, J. E. (1973b). *Education for liberation: Readings from an ideological perspective.* Upper Saddle River, NJ: Prentice Hall.

Brophy, J. E., & Good, T. L. (1986). Teacher behavior and student achievement. In M. C. Wittrock (Ed.), *Handbook of research on teaching* (3rd ed., pp. 328–375). New York: Macmillan.

Freire, P. (1971). *Pedagogy of the oppressed* (M. Bergman Ramos, Trans.). New York: Herder & Herder. (Original work published 1970)

Hutchins, R. M. (1952). *Great Books of the Western World: Vol. 1. The great conversation: The substance of a liberal education* (pp. 1–131). Chicago: Encyclopaedia Britannica.

Kliebard, H. M. (1986). *The struggle for the American curriculum: 1893–1958.* New York: Routledge.

Zeichner, K. M., & Liston, D. P. (1991). Traditions of reform in U.S. teacher education. *Journal of Teacher Education, 41,* 3–20.

INDEX